# Understanding Human Psychology

# Dr. Hoori Nadir

# Copyright



Our Social Connection

Instagram: - bphbup

Twitter: - BundelkhandPub1

YouTube: - Bundelkhand Publication House

Email:- bphbup@gmail.com

# Disclaimer

This Book **"Understanding Human Psychology"** is based on human psychology .We tried to analysis of this book free from errors. If you find any mistakes or error please tell us.

In case of any plagiarism found, the publisher will not be responsible for that. Writer will be solely responsible for her own content.

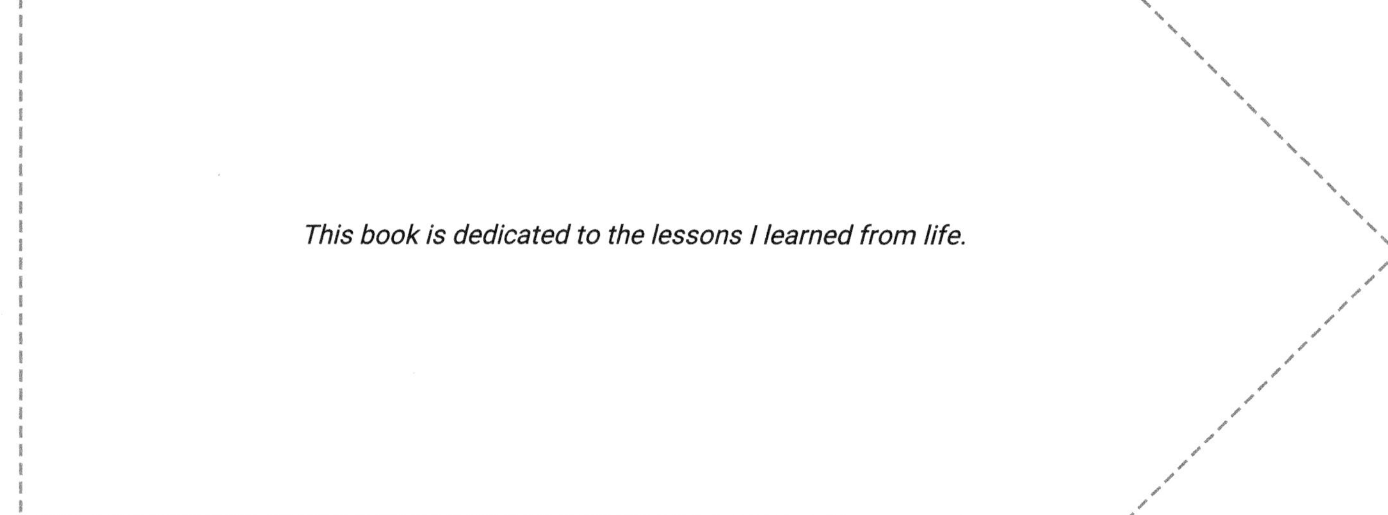

*This book is dedicated to the lessons I learned from life.*

# Acknowledgments

Writing a book on human psychology is not a solitary endeavor. It requires the support, guidance, and contribution of numerous individuals and institutions. As I reflect on the completion of this work, I am filled with gratitude towards those who have played a significant role in its fruition.

First and foremost, I express my deepest gratitude to the participants of the numerous studies, interviews, and surveys that have enriched the content of this book. Your willingness to share your experiences, thoughts, and emotions has been invaluable in shaping the understanding of human psychology presented within these pages. Without your participation, this book would not have been possible.

I extend my heartfelt appreciation to my academic mentors and advisors who have provided invaluable guidance and encouragement throughout the process of researching and writing this book. Your expertise, wisdom, and unwavering support have been instrumental in shaping the direction and content of this work. I am deeply grateful for the countless hours you have dedicated to mentoring me and for believing in the importance of this project.

I am indebted to the researchers, scholars, and authors whose groundbreaking work has paved the way for the insights and theories presented in this book. Your contributions to the field of psychology have inspired and informed my own understanding, and I am honored to build upon your work in this volume.

Special thanks are due to the editorial and production teams who have contributed their expertise and dedication to bringing this book to fruition. From manuscript preparation to publication, your professionalism and attention to detail have ensured the quality and accuracy of the final product.

I would like to express my gratitude to my colleagues and peers who have provided encouragement, feedback, and support throughout the process of writing this book. Your insights and perspectives have been invaluable in refining the ideas and arguments presented herein.

To my friends and family, who have offered unwavering love, encouragement, and understanding throughout this journey, I am deeply grateful. Your patience, support, and belief in me have sustained me through the challenges and uncertainties of writing a book, and I am profoundly thankful for your presence in my life.

Last but not least, I dedicate this book to the countless individuals who have grappled with the complexities of the human mind and spirit - those who have sought understanding, healing, and growth in the face of adversity and uncertainty. It is my hope that the insights and perspectives shared in these pages may offer solace, illumination, and inspiration to all who journey through the labyrinth of the human psyche.

In conclusion, I extend my heartfelt thanks to all who have contributed to the creation of this book. Your support, guidance, and encouragement have been invaluable, and I am deeply grateful for the opportunity to share this work with the world.

Sincerely,

**Dr. Hoori Nadir**

# Preface

Understanding the depths of human psychology is akin to exploring an endless labyrinth, where each turn leads to new revelations, complexities, and wonders. In this ever-evolving field of study, we delve into the intricate workings of the human mind, seeking to comprehend the thoughts, emotions, Behavior s, and motivations that shape our existence. It is a journey both enlightening and challenging, marked by discoveries that not only unravel the mysteries of our own psyche but also shed light on the complexities of human interaction and societal dynamics.

This book serves as a comprehensive guide to the multifaceted realm of human psychology. It is an endeavor to encapsulate the vast body of knowledge accumulated through centuries of research, observation, and introspection. From the early philosophical inquiries of ancient civilizations to the modern scientific methodologies of today, the study of human psychology has traversed a remarkable path of growth and development.

At its core, human psychology is a mosaic of diverse perspectives, theories, and approaches, each offering unique insights into the complexities of the human mind. From the psychoanalytic theories of Sigmund Freud to the Behavior ist principles of B.F. Skinner, from the cognitive revolution spearheaded by figures like Jean Piaget and Noam Chomsky to the contemporary advancements in neuroscience and evolutionary psychology, the landscape of psychological inquiry is rich with diversity and depth.

One of the fundamental aims of this book is to provide readers with a holistic understanding of human psychology, encompassing its various domains and subfields. We delve into cognitive psychology, exploring the intricacies of perception, memory, attention, and language, unraveling the mysteries of how we process information and construct our understanding of the world. We delve in to developmental psychology, tracing the journey of human growth and maturation from infancy to old age, examining the myriad factors that influence our physical, cognitive, and socioemotional development.

Moreover, we explore social psychology, investigating the intricate interplay between individuals and their social environment, delving into topics such as conformity, obedience, prejudice, and group dynamics. We examine clinical psychology, shedding light on the nature and treatment of psychological disorders, and we explore the fascinating realm of personality psychology, seeking to unravel the enduring patterns of thoughts, feelings, and Behavior s that define who we are.

However, our exploration does not stop there. We venture into the realms of positive psychology, focusing on the factors that contribute to human flourishing and well-being, and we probe into the complexities of abnormal psychology, seeking to understand the deviations from typical psychological functioning and the mechanisms underlying psychological distress.

But this book is not merely a catalog of theories and concepts. It is an invitation to embark on a journey of self-discovery and enlightenment. As readers navigate through its pages, they will encounter not only the theories and findings of scholars and researchers but also reflections on the human experience drawn from literature, art, philosophy, and everyday life. For psychology is not confined to the confines of laboratories and academic journals; it permeates every aspect of our existence, shaping our perceptions, guiding our decisions, and influencing our interactions with others.

In essence, this book is a celebration of the human mind—a testament to its complexity, resilience, and capacity for growth. It is a tribute to the individuals who have dedicated their lives to unraveling its mysteries and a call to action for future generations to continue the quest for understanding. As we embark on this journey together, let us embrace the wonder and the challenge of exploring the depths of human psychology, knowing that with each insight gained, we come closer to understanding ourselves and the world in which we live.

So, dear reader, I invite you to embark on this voyage of discovery, to open your mind to the wonders of human psychology, and to embark on a journey that will not only enrich your understanding of the human experience but also deepen your appreciation for the complexity and beauty of the human mind.

# About the writer/Proof Reader

Dr. Hoori Nadir is working as Assistant Professor in Management with BBD University, Lucknow,Uttar Pradesh. She published her research papers in journals of repute. She has been part of editorial team with different offline and online resources. She has an expertise in the field of General Management, Marketing Management,Retail Management and logistics. She had been part of numerous conferences. She is very high headed and have excellent communication and interpersonal skills. As far as the work experience is concerned, she has been associated with renowned B schools and world class Universities.

She has a passion for teaching and mentoring students.

# Index

**Table of Content**

**Page No.**

# Understanding Human Psychology:

## An Introduction

# Chapter 1:

## Exploring the Depths of Human Psychology

## Introduction

Human psychology is a vast and intricate field that delves into the inner workings of the human mind and Behavior . From the way we think, feel, and perceive the world around us to the intricacies of social interactions and emotional experiences, psychology offers valuable insights into what it means to be human. In this chapter, we will embark on a journey to explore the fundamental concepts and principles of human psychology, laying the groundwork for a deeper understanding of ourselves and others.

## The Essence of Human Psychology

At its core, human psychology seeks to unravel the mysteries of the mind—how we think, feel, and behave in various situations. It encompasses a wide range of topics, including cognition, emotion, personality, development, and social interactions. By studying these aspects of human Behavior, psychologists strive to uncover the underlying mechanisms that govern our thoughts and actions.

## Cognition: The Gateway to Understanding

Cognition, often referred to as the mental processes involved in acquiring, processing, and using information, lies at the heart of human psychology. It encompasses a myriad of functions, including perception, attention, memory, language, and problem-solving. By examining how we perceive and interpret the world around us, psychologists gain valuable insights into the intricacies of human thought processes.

## Emotion: The Driving Force Behind Behavior

Emotions play a pivotal role in shaping our Behavior and experiences. From joy and sadness to fear and anger, emotions color our perceptions and influence our decisions. Psychologists study the nature of emotions, their physiological and psychological effects, and their role in guiding adaptive Behavior s. Understanding emotions is essential for comprehending human Behavior  in various contexts, from personal relationships to societal dynamics.

## Personality: Uniqueness in Diversity

Every individual possesses a unique set of traits, Behavior s, and characteristics that define their personality. Personality psychology seeks to understand the underlying factors that contribute to the development of personality, including genetic predispositions, environmental influences, and life experiences. By studying personality traits such as extraversion, agreeableness, conscientiousness, neuroticism, and openness, psychologists gain insights into the complexities of human nature.

## Development: Nurturing Growth and Change

Human development encompasses the processes of growth, maturation, and change that occur across the lifespan. From infancy to old age, individuals undergo a series of physical, cognitive, and socioemotional transformations. Developmental psychologists study these processes, examining how genetics, environment, and social interactions shape human development. By understanding the factors that influence development, psychologists can offer valuable insights into promoting healthy growth and addressing developmental challenges.

## Social Psychology: The Power of Interactions

Humans are inherently social beings, shaped by their interactions with others. Social psychology explores the influence of social factors on individual Behavior attitudes, and beliefs. From conformity and obedience to prejudice and altruism, social psychologists investigate the dynamics of social influence and group Behavior . By studying social interactions, psychologists gain insights into the complexities of human relationships and societal dynamics.

## Essential Functions of Human Psychology

### Introduction:

Human psychology, the intricate study of the mind and Behavior, serves as a cornerstone in comprehending the complexities of human existence. It delves into the multifaceted layers of cognition, emotion, and Behavior, offering insights into the workings of the human mind. Through its various functions, human psychology illuminates the dynamics of individual and collective experiences, shaping our understanding of ourselves and the world around us.

### 1. Understanding Behavior:

One of the primary functions of human psychology is to decipher the intricacies of human Behavior. By exploring the underlying motives, thoughts, and emotions that drive actions, psychologists gain valuable insights into why individuals behave in certain ways. From basic instincts to complex social interactions, the study of Behavior sheds light on the diverse spectrum of human actions, providing a framework for understanding and predicting Behavior patterns.

## 2. Exploring Cognitive Processes:

Human psychology encompasses the examination of cognitive processes, including perception, memory, reasoning, and problem-solving. Through empirical research and theoretical frameworks, psychologists seek to unravel the mysteries of how the mind processes information and makes sense of the world. Understanding cognitive functions not only enhances our knowledge of human intelligence but also informs fields such as education, neuroscience, and artificial intelligence.

## 3. Unraveling Emotions:

Emotions play a pivotal role in human psychology, influencing Behavior  decision-making, and overall well-being. Psychologists study the nature of emotions, their physiological and psychological components, and their impact on individuals and society. By unraveling the intricacies of emotions such as happiness, sadness, fear, and anger, psychologists offer valuable insights into emotional regulation, mental health, and interpersonal relationships.

## 4. Facilitating Personal Development:

Another vital function of human psychology is to facilitate personal development and growth. Through various therapeutic approaches, psychologists assist individuals in overcoming challenges, resolving conflicts, and achieving personal goals. Whether through counseling, psychotherapy, or coaching, psychology provides tools and techniques for self-exploration, introspection, and resilience-building, empowering individuals to lead more fulfilling and meaningful lives.

## 5. Enhancing Social Understanding:

Human psychology extends beyond the individual to encompass the dynamics of social interactions and group Behavior . Social psychology investigates phenomena such as conformity, obedience, prejudice, and group dynamics, shedding light on the complexities of human relationships and societal structures. By examining the influence of social factors on individual Behavior and vice versa, psychologists contribute to our understanding of culture, identity, and social change.

## 6. Informing Decision-Making:

Psychological principles play a crucial role in informing decision-making processes across various domains, including business, public policy, and healthcare. Behavior al economics, for instance, applies psychological insights to economic decision-making, recognizing the role of cognitive biases and heuristics in shaping choices. Similarly, in fields such as marketing and advertising, an understanding of consumer psychology informs strategies aimed at influencing consumer Behavior.

# Nature and Scope of Human Psychology

## Introduction:

Human psychology is a captivating field that delves into the intricacies of the human mind and Behavior. It encompasses a broad spectrum of topics, ranging from understanding individual thoughts and emotions to unraveling complex social interactions. The nature and scope of human psychology are vast and multifaceted, offering valuable insights into what drives human Behavior and cognition.

## Nature of Human Psychology:

At its core, human psychology is the scientific study of the mind and Behavior. It seeks to explore how individuals perceive, think, feel, and act in various situations. One of the fundamental principles of psychology is that human Behavior is influenced by a combination of biological, psychological, and environmental factors.

Human psychology is inherently interdisciplinary, drawing on principles from biology, neuroscience, sociology, anthropology, and philosophy. It embraces diverse perspectives and methodologies, including experimental research, clinical observation, and theoretical modeling, to advance our understanding of human nature.

Moreover, human psychology is dynamic and ever-evolving. It adapts to new discoveries, technological advancements, and cultural changes, continuously expanding its boundaries and refining its theories.

## Scope of Human Psychology:

The scope of human psychology is vast, encompassing a wide range of subfields and applications. Some of the key areas within the scope of human psychology include:

1. **Cognitive Psychology**: Focuses on understanding mental processes such as perception, memory, language, and problem-solving. Cognitive psychologists explore how humans acquire, process, and store information, providing valuable insights into the workings of the human mind.

2. **Developmental Psychology**: Examines the psychological growth and changes that occur throughout the lifespan, from infancy to old age. Developmental psychologists study how genetics, environment, and social interactions shape human development, addressing questions about childhood development, adolescence, adulthood, and aging.

3. **Clinical Psychology**: Concerned with the diagnosis, treatment, and prevention of mental health disorders. Clinical psychologists work with individuals experiencing psychological distress or dysfunction, using various therapeutic approaches to promote mental well-being and improve quality of life.

4. **Social Psychology**: Investigates how individuals' thoughts, feelings, and Behavior s are influenced by social interactions and group dynamics. Social psychologists explore topics such as conformity, obedience, prejudice, attraction, and aggression, shedding light on the complexities of human social Behavior .

**5. Industrial-Organizational Psychology:** Applies psychological principles to the workplace, addressing issues related to employee motivation, leadership, teamwork, and organizational culture. Industrial-organizational psychologists aim to enhance organizational effectiveness and employee satisfaction through research-based interventions.

**6. Educational Psychology:** Focuses on understanding how students learn and develop within educational settings. Educational psychologists study factors that affect learning outcomes, such as teaching methods, curriculum design, student motivation, and classroom management strategies.

**7. Health Psychology:** Explores the psychological factors that influence health, illness, and healthcare Behavior . Health psychologists investigate topics such as stress, coping mechanisms, health promotion, and adherence to medical treatment, aiming to improve overall health outcomes.

## An Interdisciplinary Journey

**Introduction:**

Human psychology is a multifaceted field that delves into the complexities of the human mind, Behavior, and experiences. It is an interdisciplinary domain that draws insights from various disciplines such as neuroscience, sociology, anthropology, biology, philosophy, and even computer science. This interdisciplinary approach allows researchers and practitioners to explore the intricate workings of the human psyche from different angles, leading to a richer understanding of human Behavior and cognition.

## Neuroscience:

One of the fundamental pillars of understanding human psychology lies in neuroscience, the study of the nervous system and brain. Neuroscience provides invaluable insights into how the brain processes information, regulates emotions, and governs Behavior. Through advanced imaging techniques such as FMRI (functional magnetic resonance imaging) and EEG (electroencephalography), neuroscientists can observe brain activity in real-time, unraveling the neural mechanisms behind various psychological phenomena.

## Sociology and Anthropology:

Sociology and anthropology contribute significantly to our understanding of human psychology by examining the influence of society, culture, and environment on individual and collective Behavior. These disciplines explore how social norms, cultural practices, and social structures shape human identity, beliefs, and values. By studying diverse societies and cultures, researchers gain valuable insights into the universal and culturally specific aspects of human Behavior, shedding light on the complex interplay between nature and nurture.

## Biology:

The biological basis of human psychology is another critical area of study. Biological factors such as genetics, hormones, and neurotransmitters play a crucial role in shaping personality traits, cognitive abilities, and mental health outcomes. Genetic studies uncover hereditary predispositions to certain psychological disorders, while research on the brain's biochemistry elucidates the role of neurotransmitters like dopamine and serotonin in mood regulation and emotional processing.

## Philosophy:

Philosophy provides a conceptual framework for understanding the nature of the mind, consciousness, and reality, which are central to the study of psychology. Philosophical inquiries into topics such as free will, consciousness, and morality inform psychological theories and methodologies, guiding researchers in their quest to unravel the mysteries of human cognition and Behavior. Moreover, philosophical perspectives on ethics and morality underpin the ethical guidelines that govern psychological research and practice.

## Computer Science:

In recent years, computer science has emerged as a vital partner in advancing our understanding of human psychology. Computational models and simulations allow psychologists to test hypotheses, analyze large datasets, and simulate complex cognitive processes. Moreover, the advent of artificial intelligence and machine learning has opened new avenues for studying human Behavior  enabling researchers to develop sophisticated algorithms for tasks such as natural language processing, sentiment analysis, and facial recognition.

Human psychology is a dynamic and interdisciplinary field that benefits from the synergistic collaboration of various disciplines. By integrating insights from neuroscience, sociology, anthropology, biology, philosophy, and computer science, researchers can unravel the mysteries of the human mind and Behavior with greater depth and nuance. This interdisciplinary approach not only enriches our understanding of human psychology but also fosters innovative research and practical applications in fields ranging from mental health to artificial intelligence. As we continue to explore the complexities of the human psyche, interdisciplinary collaboration will remain essential for unlocking new insights and addressing the multifaceted challenges of the human condition.

It offers a fascinating exploration of the complexities of the human mind and Behavior. Its nature is rooted in scientific inquiry, interdisciplinary collaboration, and a dynamic pursuit of knowledge. The scope of human psychology is vast and diverse, encompassing various subfields and applications that contribute to our understanding of what it means to be human. By studying human psychology, we gain valuable insights into ourselves and others, paving the way for personal growth, social progress, and the advancement of human well-being.

Human psychology serves as a multifaceted discipline that encompasses a wide array of functions, from understanding Behavior and cognition to unraveling emotions and facilitating personal development. By exploring the intricacies of the human mind and Behavior, psychology provides valuable insights into individual and collective experiences, shaping our understanding of ourselves and the world around us. As we continue to delve deeper into the complexities of human psychology, we gain a deeper appreciation for the rich tapestry of human existence and the profound implications it holds for society.

Human psychology is a multifaceted discipline that offers valuable insights into the complexities of the human mind and Behavior. By exploring topics such as cognition, emotion, personality, development, and social interactions, psychologists seek to unravel the mysteries of human nature and enhance our understanding of ourselves and others. As we continue our journey into the depths of human psychology, we will delve deeper into these topics, uncovering the underlying mechanisms that govern our thoughts, feelings, and actions.

# Chapter 2:

## Understanding Personality: Nature, Types, and Future Implications

# Introduction

Personality, the unique combination of characteristics and traits that define an individual, has intrigued scholars, psychologists, and laypersons alike for centuries. From ancient philosophers to modern psychologists, the exploration of personality has been central to understanding human Behavior  motivations, and interactions. In this article, we delve into the nature, types, scope, functions, significance, and future implications of personality.

## Understanding the Multifaceted Nature of Personality

### Introduction:

Personality is a complex and fascinating aspect of human psychology, encompassing a wide array of traits, Behavior s, and characteristics that define who we are as individuals. It influences how we interact with others, perceive the world around us, and navigate through life's challenges. Exploring the nature of personality unveils its intricate layers, shedding light on its origins, development, and impact on various aspects of human experience.

### The Nature of Personality:

At its core, personality refers to the unique pattern of thoughts, feelings, and Behavior s that distinguish one person from another. It encompasses both stable traits and dynamic states, influenced by genetic predispositions, environmental factors, and individual experiences. Psychologists have proposed various theories to understand the nature of personality, each offering valuable insights into its complexities.

## Trait Theory:

Trait theory posits that personality can be described in terms of a set of enduring traits or characteristics that remain relatively stable over time and across different situations. These traits, such as extraversion, agreeableness, conscientiousness, neuroticism, and openness to experience, form the building blocks of an individual's personality profile. Trait theorists believe that these fundamental dimensions capture the essential features of human personality and shape Behavior across diverse contexts.

## Psychodynamic Theory:

Developed by Sigmund Freud, psychodynamic theory emphasizes the role of unconscious processes in shaping personality. According to Freud, personality is structured into three levels: the id, ego, and superego. The id operates on the pleasure principle, seeking immediate gratification of basic impulses and desires. The ego functions as the rational mediator between the id and the external world, while the superego represents internalized societal and moral standards. Psychodynamic theorists believe that conflicts between these psychological forces influence personality development and Behavior.

## Behavior al Theory:

Behavior al theory focuses on observable Behavior s and the environmental factors that shape them. It suggests that personality is largely a product of conditioning and reinforcement, with Behavior s learned through interactions with the environment. Behavior ists emphasize the importance of environmental stimuli and reinforcement schedules in shaping personality traits and Behavior al patterns. This perspective highlights the role of learning processes, such as classical and operant conditioning, in molding individual differences in personality.

## Humanistic Theory:

Humanistic theory emphasizes the inherent drive towards self-actualization and personal growth. Pioneered by psychologists like Abraham Maslow and Carl Rogers, this approach views personality development as a quest for fulfillment and authenticity. Humanistic theorists emphasize the importance of subjective experiences, personal values, and the pursuit of meaningful goals in shaping personality. They believe that individuals have the capacity to consciously choose their paths in life and strive towards realizing their full potential.

## Biopsychosocial Perspective:

The biopsychosocial perspective integrates biological, psychological, and social factors in understanding personality. It recognizes the interplay between genetic predispositions, neurobiological processes, cognitive factors, interpersonal relationships, and cultural influences in shaping individual differences in personality. This holistic approach acknowledges the complex interactions between nature and nurture, highlighting the dynamic nature of personality development.

The nature of personality is a multifaceted phenomenon, influenced by a myriad of factors spanning genetics, environment, cognition, and social dynamics. From trait theory to psychodynamic perspectives, each theoretical framework offers valuable insights into the intricacies of human personality. Understanding the nature of personality not only enriches our comprehension of individual differences but also informs interventions aimed at fostering personal growth, improving interpersonal relationships, and enhancing overall well-being. By exploring the diverse dimensions of personality, we gain deeper insight into what makes each of us unique.

# Understanding A and B Personality Types:

## How They Shape Behavior and Success

Personality psychology has long been a fascinating field of study, exploring the diverse ways individuals perceive, interact with, and navigate the world around them. Among the many frameworks used to understand personality, the A and B personality types stand out for their distinct characteristics and implications for various aspects of life.

Coined by cardiologists Meyer Friedman and Ray Rosenman in the 1950s, the A and B personality types were initially linked to the risk of coronary heart disease. However, over time, researchers have expanded their focus to explore how these personality types influence Behavior, relationships, and even career success.

Let's delve into the defining traits of A and B personalities:

## A. Personality Type:

**1. Competitive Nature**: Individuals with an A personality type are often characterized by their competitive drive. They thrive in environments where they can set goals, take charge, and strive for excellence. This drive can propel them to success in their careers and personal endeavors.

**2. Sense of Urgency**: A personalities tend to have a heightened sense of urgency. They are often seen as fast-paced and impatient, preferring to tackle tasks quickly and efficiently. While this trait can lead to productivity, it may also result in stress and burnout if not managed effectively.

**3. Highly Organized**: Organization is a hallmark trait of A personalities. They prefer structure and order in their lives, often planning their days meticulously to maximize productivity. This tendency towards organization can make them reliable and efficient team members.

**4. Impatience with Delays**: Individuals with an A personality type can become frustrated by delays or inefficiencies. They prefer to see immediate results and may struggle with patience when progress is slower than anticipated.

**B. Personality Type:**

**1. Relaxed Demeanor**: In contrast to A personalities, B personalities have a more relaxed and laid-back approach to life. They tend to go with the flow and are comfortable adapting to changing circumstances. This flexibility can be advantageous in unpredictable environments.

**2. Creative and Imaginative**: B personalities often possess a creative streak, enjoying activities that allow them to express their imagination and explore new ideas. They may thrive in roles that require innovation and out-of-the-box thinking.

**3. Tolerance for Ambiguity**: Unlike their A counterparts, B personalities are typically more tolerant of ambiguity and uncertainty. They are comfortable navigating situations where the outcome is unclear, preferring to trust in their ability to adapt as needed.

**4. Strong Interpersonal Skills**: B personalities excel in interpersonal relationships, often demonstrating empathy, patience, and active listening skills. They prioritize building connections with others and fostering a supportive environment.

### ... Implications for Success:

Both A and B personality types bring unique strengths to the table, and understanding these differences can be instrumental in achieving success:

- ..**Career Fit**..: A personalities may excel in high-pressure environments such as sales or leadership roles, where their competitive drive and organizational skills are valued. On the other hand, B personalities may thrive in creative fields like design or marketing, where their imaginative thinking shines.

- ..**Team Dynamics**..: Recognizing the diverse personality types within a team can enhance collaboration and productivity. A balanced team comprising both A and B personalities can leverage the strengths of each individual while mitigating potential conflicts.

- ..**Personal Growth**..: Regardless of personality type, self-awareness is key to personal growth and development. Individuals can harness the strengths of their personality type while actively working to mitigate potential weaknesses, leading to greater fulfillment and success in both professional and personal spheres.

In conclusion, the A and B personality types offer valuable insights into human Behavior and how individuals approach various aspects of life. By understanding and embracing these differences, we can cultivate environments that foster collaboration, creativity, and ultimately, success.

## Personality and Interpersonal Skills in the Contemporary Landscape

In the ever-evolving realm of human interaction, the dynamics of personality and interpersonal skills have emerged as quintessential facets shaping individual success and societal harmony. However, amidst the cacophony of scholarly discourse and practical application, a lurking shadow looms-plagiarism. The appropriation of ideas, thoughts, and insights without proper attribution not only tarnishes academic integrity but also undermines the essence of genuine intellectual discourse. Thus, it becomes imperative to dissect this phenomenon concerning the pivotal domains of personality and interpersonal skills.

Personality, the unique amalgamation of traits, Behavior s, and attitudes, serves as the bedrock upon which interpersonal interactions are built. From the effervescent extrovert to the introspective introvert, the spectrum of personalities dictates how individuals perceive and respond to the world around them. However, the temptation to plagiarize in discussions on personality can be insidious. Scholars and practitioners, eager to bolster their theories or pedagogical approaches, may succumb to the allure of borrowing without acknowledgment. Yet, this erodes the very essence of originality that fuels advancements in psychological understanding.

Similarly, the terrain of interpersonal skills, encompassing communication, empathy, and conflict resolution, is fertile ground for the propagation of plagiarized ideas. In a society that lionizes charisma and eloquence, individuals may resort to appropriating others' communication techniques or conflict resolution strategies without due credit. The consequences are manifold—a dilution of authentic human connection, a stunting of personal growth, and a corrosion of trust within interpersonal relationships.

To mitigate the proliferation of plagiarism in discussions on personality and interpersonal skills, concerted efforts must be undertaken at both individual and institutional levels. Educators bear the responsibility of nurturing a culture of academic integrity, instilling in students the value of original thought and proper citation. Moreover, fostering critical thinking skills equips learners with the discernment to distinguish between genuine contributions and derivative imitations.

Furthermore, scholars and practitioners must lead by example, upholding rigorous standards of attribution in their research and professional endeavors. By championing transparency and acknowledgment of intellectual debts, they cultivate an environment conducive to genuine collaboration and innovation. Additionally, the integration of plagiarism detection software serves as a deterrent against academic dishonesty, safeguarding the integrity of scholarly discourse.

The nexus of personality and interpersonal skills stands as a bastion of human understanding and societal cohesion. Yet, the specter of plagiarism threatens to erode the foundation upon which these domains are built. Only through a steadfast commitment to academic integrity and ethical conduct can we navigate this labyrinthine landscape, forging a future where originality and authenticity reign supreme.

# Enhancing Your Personality:
# Practical Tips for Personal Growth

In the journey of life, our personalities serve as the lens through which we interact with the world. A vibrant and well-rounded personality can enrich our experiences, foster deeper connections, and open doors to opportunities. While personality traits are often seen as inherent, they are also malleable, subject to change and development through conscious effort and practice. Whether you're looking to boost your confidence, become more charismatic, or cultivate greater resilience, enhancing your personality is within reach with the right strategies. Here are some practical tips to help you embark on the path of personal growth and enhance your personality:

## 1. Self-Reflection and Awareness

The first step towards enhancing your personality is to develop self-awareness. Take time to reflect on your strengths, weaknesses, values, and beliefs. Journaling, meditation, or engaging in introspective activities can help you gain clarity about who you are and what you aspire to become. Pay attention to your thoughts, emotions, and Behavior s in various situations to identify patterns and areas for improvement.

## 2. Set Clear Goals

Define specific goals related to the aspects of your personality you wish to enhance. Whether it's improving communication skills, becoming more assertive, or fostering a positive mindset, setting clear and achievable objectives provides direction and motivation. Break down larger goals into smaller, actionable steps, and track your progress along the way. Celebrate your achievements, no matter how small, to stay motivated and committed to your growth journey.

### 3. Continuous Learning and Development

Embrace a growth mindset that views challenges as opportunities for learning and improvement. Seek out opportunities for personal and professional development, such as attending workshops, taking courses, or reading books on topics that interest you. Surround yourself with people who inspire you and challenge you to grow. Be open to feedback from others and use it as constructive input for self-improvement.

### 4. Cultivate Positive Habits

Your habits shape your personality and Behavior. Cultivate habits that align with the traits you want to enhance. For example, practice gratitude daily to foster a positive outlook, engage in regular exercise to boost your confidence and well-being, and prioritize self-care to maintain balance and resilience. Be mindful of negative habits that may hinder your growth, and work on replacing them with more constructive alternatives.

### 5. Develop Empathy and Emotional Intelligence

Enhancing your personality also involves improving your ability to understand and connect with others. Cultivate empathy by putting yourself in others' shoes and seeking to understand their perspectives and feelings. Develop emotional intelligence by being aware of your own emotions and how they influence your Behavior  as well as recognizing and managing the emotions of others effectively.

### 6. Practice Effective Communication

Effective communication is essential for building meaningful relationships and expressing yourself authentically. Practice active listening, maintain eye contact, and communicate clearly and assertively. Pay attention to your body language and tone of voice, as they convey as much, if not more, than your words. Learn to express your thoughts and feelings openly and respectfully, while also being receptive to the viewpoints of others.

## 7. Step Out of Your Comfort Zone

Personal growth often occurs outside of your comfort zone. Challenge yourself to try new experiences, take on unfamiliar tasks, and confront your fears. By pushing past your limitations, you'll discover new strengths and capabilities that contribute to your personal development. Embrace failure as a natural part of the learning process and use it as an opportunity to adapt and grow stronger.

## 8. Practice Authenticity

Authenticity is the cornerstone of a magnetic personality. Be true to yourself, embrace your uniqueness, and let your genuine self shine through. Avoid trying to imitate others or conforming to societal expectations at the expense of your authenticity. When you embrace who you are fully, you'll attract people who appreciate and resonate with your true essence.

## Conclusion

Enhancing your personality is a lifelong journey that requires dedication, self-awareness, and a willingness to step out of your comfort zone. By setting clear goals, cultivating positive habits, and continuously learning and growing, you can unlock your full potential and become the best version of yourself. Remember that personal growth is not a destination but a continual process of evolution and self-discovery. Embrace the journey, celebrate your progress, and enjoy the transformation that comes with enhancing your personality.

# Chapter 3:

Emotions..The Complex World of Emotions:
Understanding the Heart of Human Experience..

Emotions are the colors that paint the canvas of human experience. They are the whispers of our soul, the guiding forces behind our actions, and the essence of what makes us uniquely human. From the exhilarating heights of joy to the depths of sorrow, emotions weave through every aspect of our lives, shaping our perceptions, decisions, and relationships.

## ..The Nature of Emotions...

At their core, emotions are complex physiological and psychological responses to stimuli, both internal and external. They are the product of intricate interactions between our brains, hormones, and nervous systems. While some emotions are innate and universal across cultures, such as happiness, fear, anger, and sadness, others are influenced by individual experiences, upbringing, and societal norms.

## ..The Emotional Spectrum...

The emotional spectrum is vast and multifaceted, encompassing a wide range of feelings, each with its own distinct flavor and intensity. Love, for instance, can manifest as tender affection, passionate desire, or profound attachment. Similarly, anger may range from mild irritation to explosive rage, depending on the circumstances.

## ..The Role of Emotions in Human Life...

Emotions serve as our compass, guiding us through the labyrinth of existence. They provide valuable insights into our needs, desires, and values, helping us navigate the complexities of social interactions and personal relationships. Joy motivates us to pursue activities that bring us pleasure and fulfillment, while fear alerts us to potential threats and dangers. Without emotions, life would be devoid of meaning and purpose, akin to navigating a ship without a compass in a vast, uncharted sea.

## ..The Power of Emotional Intelligence...

Emotional intelligence (EI) is the ability to recognize, understand, and manage both our own emotions and those of others. It is a crucial skill that enables us to communicate effectively, build strong interpersonal connections, and navigate conflicts constructively. Individuals with high EI are better equipped to cope with stress, adapt to change, and lead fulfilling lives.

## ..Emotions and Mental Health...

While emotions are a natural and essential part of the human experience, imbalances or disturbances in emotional regulation can lead to mental health issues such as depression, anxiety, and mood disorders. It is important to acknowledge and validate our emotions, rather than suppress or ignore them, as repressed feelings can manifest in harmful ways, both psychologically and physically.

## ..Cultivating Emotional Well-being...

Cultivating emotional well-being requires self-awareness, self-compassion, and a willingness to engage in introspection. Practices such as mindfulness meditation, journaling, and therapy can help individuals develop greater emotional resilience and self-regulation. Building strong support networks and fostering meaningful connections with others are also vital components of emotional well-being.

In the tapestry of human existence, emotions are the threads that bind us together, weaving a rich tapestry of experiences, memories, and relationships. By embracing our emotions with openness and curiosity, we can embark on a journey of self-discovery and personal growth, enriching our lives and the lives of those around us. Emotions are not merely fleeting sensations; they are the essence of what it means to be human.

# Nature of Emotions

## ..Exploring the Intricate Nature of Emotions: Understanding the Human Experience...

Emotions are the cornerstone of the human experience, shaping our perceptions, actions, and relationships. From the euphoria of joy to the depths of despair, emotions color every facet of our lives, providing richness and depth to our existence. Yet, despite their omnipresence, the nature of emotions remains a subject of profound fascination and inquiry.

### ..The Complexity of Emotions...

At their essence, emotions are complex psychological and physiological responses to stimuli, both internal and external. They arise from a myriad of sources, including our thoughts, experiences, and biochemical processes within the brain. This intricate interplay between cognition, biology, and environment gives rise to the diverse range of emotions that human's experience.

## ..The Role of Evolution...

From an evolutionary standpoint, emotions have played a crucial role in human survival and adaptation. Fear, for example, triggers the body's "fight or flight" response, enabling us to respond quickly to threats and dangers in our environment. Similarly, feelings of love and attachment foster social bonds and cooperation, enhancing our chances of survival within communities.

## ..Cultural and Individual Variability…

While there are universal aspects to emotions, their expression and interpretation vary across cultures and individuals. Cultural norms, values, and socialization practices influence how emotions are perceived and expressed. Moreover, individual differences in personality, temperament, and life experiences shape our emotional responses to different situations.

## ..The Dual Nature of Emotions…

Emotions can be both adaptive and maladaptive, depending on the context in which they occur. Positive emotions, such as happiness and gratitude, enhance our well-being and resilience, fostering psychological growth and interpersonal connections. Conversely, negative emotions, such as anger and sadness, can signal unmet needs or threats to our well-being, prompting us to take corrective action.

## ..The Importance of Emotional Regulation...

Effective emotional regulation is essential for maintaining psychological health and functioning. It involves the ability to recognize, understand, and manage one's own emotions in a constructive manner. Strategies such as cognitive reappraisal, mindfulness, and social support can help individuals modulate their emotional responses and cope with stressors more effectively.

## ..The Link between Emotions and Health...

Mounting evidence suggests that emotions exert a profound influence on physical health and well-being. Chronic stress, for instance, has been linked to a host of health problems, including cardiovascular disease, immune dysfunction, and mental illness. Conversely, positive emotions have been associated with better health outcomes, including reduced inflammation, improved immune function, and enhanced longevity.

## ..Emotions in the Digital Age...

In today's digital age, the landscape of human emotions is evolving in unprecedented ways. Social media platforms, for example, have transformed the dynamics of social interaction, providing new avenues for self-expression and connection. However, they also present challenges, such as the proliferation of cyber bullying and the pressure to maintain a curate online persona.

## ..The Future of Emotional Science...

As our understanding of emotions continues to deepen, so too does our appreciation for their profound influence on human Behavior and society at large. Advances in neuroscience, psychology, and technology offer exciting opportunities to unravel the mysteries of emotions and develop innovative interventions to promote emotional well-being.

In conclusion, the nature of emotions is a multifaceted phenomenon that defies easy categorization. From their evolutionary origins to their role in shaping human Behavior, emotions remain a rich and fertile area of inquiry. By exploring the intricacies of emotions, we gain valuable insights into what it means to be human and how we can navigate the complexities of our emotional landscape with greater wisdom and compassion.

## Significance of emotional well being

## Nurturing Emotional Well-Being: A Holistic Approach to Mental Health

In the pursuit of a fulfilling life, we often focus on tangible achievements like career success, financial stability, and physical health. However, one aspect that is frequently overlooked but equally crucial is emotional well -being.

Emotional well-being encompasses a spectrum of feelings, from happiness and contentment to stress and sadness. It's about how we perceive ourselves, manage our emotions, cope with challenges, and cultivate positive relationships. Just as physical health requires attention and care, nurturing emotional well-being is essential for leading a balanced and satisfying life.

### ... Understanding Emotional Well-Being

Emotional well-being is more than just the absence of negative emotions; it involves actively cultivating positive ones. It's about building resilience, self-awareness, and the ability to navigate life's ups and downs with grace and equanimity.

**1...Self-Awareness..**: Understanding our emotions, thoughts, and Behavior s is the cornerstone of emotional well-being. It involves being in tune with our feelings, recognizing triggers, and understanding how our emotions impact our actions.

**2...Resilience..**: Resilience is the ability to bounce back from adversity. It's about facing challenges with optimism, learning from setbacks, and adapting to change. Cultivating resilience involves building a strong support network, maintaining a positive outlook, and developing problem-solving skills.

**3...Emotional Regulation..**: Emotions are a natural part of being human, but it's essential to regulate them effectively. This means managing stress, anger, anxiety, and other negative emotions in healthy ways, such as practicing mindfulness, deep breathing, or engaging in hobbies that bring joy.

**4...Connection..**: Humans are social beings, and meaningful connections with others are vital for emotional well-being. Whether it's family, friends, or community, fostering supportive relationships provides a sense of belonging, love, and validation.

## ... Practices for Cultivating Emotional Well-Being

**1...Mindfulness and Meditation..**: Mindfulness practices, such as meditation, help cultivate self-awareness and presence. They teach us to observe our thoughts and emotions without judgment, fostering a sense of calm and inner peace.

**2...Physical Activity..**: Regular exercise not only benefits physical health but also has a profound impact on emotional well-being. Physical activity releases endorphins, the body's natural mood lifters, and reduces stress hormones like cortisol.

**3...Healthy Lifestyle Choices..:** Eating a balanced diet, getting enough sleep, and avoiding harmful substances like drugs and alcohol are essential for overall well-being, including emotional health.

**4 ...Expressive Arts..:** Engaging in creative activities like painting, writing, or music can be therapeutic and provide an outlet for self-expression. These activities allow us to explore our emotions in a safe and constructive way.

**5...Seeking Support..:** It's okay to ask for help when needed. Whether it's talking to a trusted friend, seeking therapy, or joining a support group, reaching out for support can provide perspective, validation, and guidance during challenging times.

## ... The Importance of Emotional Well-Being in Today's World

In today's fast-paced and often stressful world, prioritizing emotional well-being is more important than ever. The pressures of work, social media, and societal expectations can take a toll on our mental health if left unchecked.

By investing in emotional well-being, individuals can experience greater resilience, happiness, and overall life satisfaction. They are better equipped to handle stress, navigate relationships, and pursue their goals with clarity and purpose.

Furthermore, when individuals prioritize their emotional well-being, it has a ripple effect on society as a whole. Healthy and emotionally balanced individuals contribute positively to their communities, fostering empathy, cooperation, and social harmony.

Emotional well-being is a fundamental aspect of overall health and happiness. By nurturing our emotional selves through self-awareness, resilience, connection, and healthy practices, we can lead more fulfilling and meaningful lives.

In a world where mental health challenges are increasingly prevalent, it's essential to prioritize emotional well-being and create a culture that value and supports mental health for all. Remember, taking care of your emotional health is not selfish; it's an act of self-love and empowerment that benefits both individuals and society as a whole.

How to overcome emotional imbalance

Finding Balance: Remedial Measures for Emotional Imbalance

In the tumultuous journey of life, emotional imbalance can often disrupt our sense of harmony and well-being. Whether it's stress, anxiety, depression, or any other emotional challenge, finding equilibrium becomes paramount for leading a fulfilling life. Fortunately, there are various remedial measures one can undertake to restore emotional balance and cultivate resilience.

## ... Understanding Emotional Imbalance

Emotions are an integral part of human experience, serving as signals that provide insight into our inner state and external circumstances. However, when emotions become overwhelming or prolonged, they can lead to imbalance, affecting mental health and overall quality of life.

Common signs of emotional imbalance include:

1...**Mood Swings**:.. Fluctuations between extreme highs and lows.

2...**Persistent Anxiety or Stress**:.. Constant worry or tension without apparent cause.

3...**Feelings of Sadness or Hopelessness**:.. Prolonged periods of low mood or despair.

4....**Irritability or Anger**: Reacting excessively to minor triggers.

5. ...**Difficulty Concentrating**:.. Inability to focus due to racing thoughts or preoccupation with emotions.

## ... Remedial Measures for Emotional Imbalance

1...**Mindfulness and Meditation**: Practicing mindfulness can help in cultivating awareness of one's thoughts and emotions without judgment. Meditation techniques such as deep breathing, body scans, or guided imagery can promote relaxation and emotional stability.

**2...Regular Exercise**: Physical activity releases endorphins, neurotransmitters that boost mood and reduce stress. Aim for at least 30 minutes of moderate exercise most days of the week to experience its mood-enhancing benefits.

**3...Healthy Lifestyle Choices**: Maintain a balanced diet, prioritize sufficient sleep, and avoid excessive alcohol or substance use. Nourishing your body with nutritious food and adequate rest can significantly impact your emotional well-being.

**4 …Seeking Support**: Don't hesitate to reach out to friends, family, or a professional therapist for support. Talking about your emotions can provide validation and perspective, while therapy offers tools and strategies to manage them effectively.

**5...Journaling: Expressing** thoughts and emotions through writing can be therapeutic. Keep a journal to track your feelings, identify patterns, and explore underlying causes of emotional imbalance.

**6...Setting Boundaries**: Learn to recognize and assert your limits in personal and professional relationships. Establishing healthy boundaries protects your emotional energy and fosters mutual respect.

**7...Engaging in Creative Outlets**: Channel your emotions into creative pursuits such as art, music, or writing. Creative expression serves as a cathartic outlet for processing emotions and fostering self-discovery.

**8...Cognitive Behavior al Techniques**: Challenge negative thought patterns and replace them with more rational and constructive ones. Cognitive-Behavior al therapy (CBT) techniques teach skills to reframe perspectives and develop coping mechanisms.

**9...Mind-Body Practices**: Explore holistic approaches such as yoga, tai chi, or acupuncture to harmonize mind and body. These practices combine physical movement with mindfulness, promoting relaxation and emotional equilibrium.

**10...Self-Compassion**: Practice kindness and understanding towards yourself, especially during times of emotional distress. Treat yourself with the same compassion you would offer to a friend facing similar challenges.

## ... Conclusion

Emotional imbalance is a natural aspect of the human experience, but it doesn't have to dictate the course of our lives. By incorporating remedial measures such as mindfulness, exercise, seeking support, and self-compassion, we can navigate through emotional turbulence with resilience and grace. Remember, finding balance is an ongoing journey, and each step taken towards emotional well-being is a testament to our strength and courage.

# Chapter 4:

## Motivation

## Unveiling the Essence of Motivation: Igniting the Flame Within

## Introduction:

Motivation, the driving force behind human action, is a complex amalgamation of internal and external factors that ignite the flame of ambition within individuals. It's the invisible hand guiding us towards our goals, propelling us through challenges, and inspiring us to reach new heights. In the intricate tapestry of human psychology, understanding motivation unravels pathways to personal and professional fulfillment. Let's embark on a journey to explore the essence of motivation and unlock its transformative power.

## The Anatomy of Motivation:

At its core, motivation encompasses a myriad of psychological processes influenced by biological, social, and environmental factors. Psychologists often categorize motivation into intrinsic and extrinsic forms. Intrinsic motivation arises from internal desires, passions, and the inherent enjoyment of an activity itself, while extrinsic motivation stems from external rewards or pressures.

Intrinsic motivation is like a spark of creativity that fuels artistic endeavors, the drive for mastery that pushes athletes to their limits, or the satisfaction derived from solving a challenging problem. It's deeply intertwined with autonomy, competence, and relatedness, as proposed by Self-Determination Theory, highlighting the importance of feeling in control, competent, and connected to others in fostering intrinsic motivation.

Conversely, extrinsic motivation manifests in the form of tangible rewards, such as money, fame, or praise, as well as social expectations or obligations. While external incentives can kickstart Behavior  their effectiveness often wanes over time, especially if intrinsic motivation is lacking. However, when aligned with intrinsic motives, extrinsic rewards can complement and enhance motivation, creating a synergistic effect.

## The Dynamics of Motivation:

Motivation is not a static entity but a dynamic force influenced by various internal and external factors. The Expectancy-Value Theory emphasizes the importance of belief in one's ability to achieve a goal (expectancy) and the perceived value of that goal (value) in driving motivation. When individuals believe they can succeed and attach significance to the outcome, their motivation soars.

Furthermore, the Achievement Goal Theory distinguishes between mastery-oriented and performance-oriented goals. Mastery goals focus on personal development, learning, and mastery of skills, fostering intrinsic motivation and resilience in the face of setbacks. In contrast, performance goals center on outperforming others or demonstrating competence, often leading to a fixation on outcomes and a fear of failure.

## The Role of Emotion and Mindset:

Emotions play a pivotal role in motivation, serving as potent catalysts or barriers to action. Positive emotions like enthusiasm, passion, and joy propel individuals forward, while negative emotions such as fear, anxiety, or self-doubt can paralyze progress. Cultivating emotional intelligence, self-awareness, and resilience equips individuals with the tools to navigate the turbulent seas of motivation.

Moreover, mindset, as delineated by Carol Dweck's Growth Mindset theory, profoundly influences motivation and achievement. A growth mindset, characterized by a belief in the malleability of abilities and a focus on learning and development, fosters resilience, perseverance, and a willingness to embrace challenges. In contrast, a fixed mindset, driven by the belief in innate talent and a fear of failure, stifles motivation and impedes growth.

## Strategies for Cultivating Motivation:

Unlocking sustained motivation requires a multifaceted approach that addresses both intrinsic and extrinsic factors while nurturing a growth-oriented mindset. Here are some strategies to cultivate and sustain motivation:

**1. Set Clear and Meaningful Goals**: Establish specific, challenging, and personally meaningful goals that align with your values and aspirations.

**2. Foster Autonomy and Mastery**: Seek opportunities for self-directed learning, skill development, and personal growth to foster a sense of autonomy and competence.

**3. Cultivate a Growth Mindset**: Embrace challenges, learn from failures, and cultivate a belief in the power of effort and perseverance to fuel long-term motivation.

**4. Create a Supportive Environment**: Surround yourself with positive influences, supportive peers, mentors, and role models who encourage and inspire you.

**5. Celebrate Progress**: Acknowledge and celebrate small wins along the journey, reinforcing a sense of accomplishment and momentum.

Motivation, the invisible force driving human Behavior, holds the key to unlocking our full potential and realizing our dreams. By understanding the intricacies of motivation and harnessing its transformative power, we can embark on a journey of personal and professional growth, fueled by passion, purpose, and perseverance. So, ignite the flame within, and let motivation propel you towards a future brimming with possibilities.

## Theories of Motivation

Exploring the theories of motivation delves into the complex interplay of factors that drive human Behavior. From basic survival instincts to higher-level psychological needs, understanding what motivates individuals is fundamental to fields ranging from psychology to business management. In this extensive exploration, we will elaborate on several prominent theories of motivation, including Maslow's Hierarchy of Needs, Herzberg's Two-Factor Theory, Expectancy Theory, and Self-Determination Theory, among others.

### 1...Maslow's Hierarchy of Needs..:

Maslow's Hierarchy of Needs, proposed by Abraham Maslow in 1943, is one of the most well-known theories of motivation. The theory suggests that individuals are motivated to fulfill a hierarchy of needs, with basic physiological needs at the bottom and higher-order needs at the top. The hierarchy consists of five levels:

- ..**Physiological needs**..: These are the basic requirements for human survival, such as food, water, and shelter.

- ..**Safety needs**..: Once physiological needs are met, individuals seek safety and security, including financial security, health, and protection from physical harm.

- ..**Love and belongingness needs**..: After safety needs are satisfied, people crave love, friendship, and a sense of belonging.

- ..**Esteem needs**..: Once social needs are fulfilled, individuals desire recognition, respect, and self-esteem from others.

- ..**Self-actualization**..: At the top of the hierarchy is self-actualization, where individuals seek personal growth, self-fulfillment, and realizing their full potential.

Maslow's theory suggests that individuals progress through these levels sequentially, with higher-order needs becoming motivators once lower-level needs are satisfied. However, critics argue that the hierarchy may not apply universally across cultures and that individuals may pursue multiple needs simultaneously.


**2...Herzberg's Two-Factor Theory..:**


Herzberg's Two-Factor Theory, proposed by Frederick Herzberg in the 1950s, distinguishes between two types of factors that influence motivation and job satisfaction: hygiene factors and motivators. Hygiene factors are related to the work environment and include factors such as salary, working conditions, and company policies. According to Herzberg, these factors do not directly motivate employees but can lead to dissatisfaction if not adequately addressed. On the other hand, motivators are intrinsic to the job itself and include factors such as recognition, responsibility, and opportunities for personal growth. Herzberg argued that these factors directly contribute to job satisfaction and motivation.

## 3...Expectancy Theory..:

Expectancy Theory, proposed by Victor Vroom in the 1960s, posits that individuals are motivated to act in certain ways based on their expectations of the outcomes of their actions. The theory suggests that motivation depends on three factors:

- ..**Expectancy**..: The belief that effort will lead to performance. Individuals assess whether they have the necessary skills and resources to achieve a desired outcome.

- ..**Instrumentality**..: The belief that performance will lead to outcomes or rewards. Individuals evaluate whether achieving a certain level of performance will result in desired rewards.

- ..**Valence**..: The value or attractiveness of the outcomes or rewards. Individuals assess the personal importance or desirability of the rewards associated with a particular outcome.

According to Expectancy Theory, individuals are most motivated when they believe that their efforts will lead to successful performance and desirable outcomes.

## 4...Self-Determination Theory..:

Self-Determination Theory, proposed by Edward Deci and Richard Ryan in the 1980s, focuses on the role of intrinsic and extrinsic motivation in driving Behavior. The theory distinguishes between intrinsic motivation, which arises from internal factors such as personal interest and enjoyment, and extrinsic motivation, which arises from external factors such as rewards and punishments.

Self-Determination Theory posits that intrinsic motivation is the most effective driver of Behavior, as it leads to greater satisfaction, creativity, and persistence. However, extrinsic motivators can also influence Behavior, particularly when they support individuals' intrinsic motivation or when intrinsic motivation is low.

The theory also emphasizes the importance of three basic psychological needs:

- ..**Autonomy**..: The need to feel in control of one's own actions and choices.

- ..**Competence**..: The need to feel capable and effective in one's activities.

- ..**Relatedness**..: The need to feel connected to others and to experience a sense of belongingness and intimacy.

According to Self-Determination Theory, satisfying these needs is essential for fostering intrinsic motivation and psychological well-being.

**5....Goal-Setting Theory..:**

Goal-Setting Theory, proposed by Edwin Locke and Gary Latham in the 1960s and 1970s, highlights the importance of setting specific and challenging goals in motivating individuals. According to the theory, clear and ambitious goals provide direction, focus attention, and stimulate effort. Additionally, feedback on progress toward goal attainment is crucial for maintaining motivation and adjusting strategies as needed.

The theory identifies five key principles of effective goal setting:

- ..**Clarity**..: Goals should be clear and unambiguous, with a precise description of what is to be accomplished.

- ..**Challenge**..: Goals should be challenging but attainable, stretching individuals to exert effort and develop their skills.

- ..**Commitment**..: Individuals should be committed to their goals and actively engaged in pursuing them.

- ..**Feedback**..: Regular feedback on progress toward goal attainment helps individuals stay motivated and adjusts their efforts as needed.

- ..**Task complexity**..: Goals should match the complexity of the task and individuals' skills, ensuring that they are neither too easy nor too difficult to achieve.

By understanding these principles, organizations can harness the power of goal setting to motivate employees and improve performance.

## 6...Cognitive Evaluation Theory..:

Cognitive Evaluation Theory, an extension of Self-Determination Theory, focuses on the impact of extrinsic rewards on intrinsic motivation. According to the theory, providing extrinsic rewards for activities that individuals already find intrinsically motivating can undermine their intrinsic motivation by reducing their sense of autonomy and competence. On the other hand, rewards that support individuals' intrinsic motivation, such as positive feedback and recognition, can enhance intrinsic motivation and performance.

The theory suggests that the manner in which rewards are delivered, as well as the perceived locus of causality (internal vs. external), influences their impact on intrinsic motivation. For example, rewards that are perceived as controlling or coercive may undermine intrinsic motivation, whereas rewards that are perceived as informational or supportive may enhance intrinsic motivation.

## 7...Reinforcement Theory..:

Reinforcement Theory, also known as operant conditioning theory, was developed by B.F. Skinner in the mid-20th century. The theory posits that Behavior  is influenced by its consequences, with Behavior s that are reinforced tending to be repeated and Behavior s that are punished or not reinforced tending to diminish.

Reinforcement can be positive, involving the presentation of a desirable stimulus following a Behavior  or negative, involving the removal of an aversive stimulus following a Behavior . Additionally, reinforcement can be continuous, occurring after every instance of the Behavior, or intermittent, occurring after some but not all instances of the Behavior.

By understanding the principles of reinforcement, organizations can design reward systems and incentives that encourage desired Behavior s and discourage undesirable Behavior s.

In conclusion, the theories of motivation offer valuable insights into the complex factors that drive human Behavior . From basic survival instincts to higher-level psychological needs, individuals are motivated by a variety of factors that interact in intricate ways. By understanding these theories and their implications, organizations can better motivate their employees, enhance job satisfaction, and improve performance.

Remedial measures for demotivated people

Motivating demotivated individuals can be a delicate process, as everyone's reasons for feeling demotivated can vary. Here are some general strategies and remedies that can help:

1...**Listen and Understand**..: Take the time to listen to their concerns and understand why they are feeling demotivated. Sometimes just having someone to talk to can make a big difference.

2...**Set Achievable Goals**..: Help them break down their tasks into smaller, more manageable goals. Achieving these smaller goals can provide a sense of accomplishment and motivation to tackle bigger challenges.

3....**Provide Support**..: Offer your support and encouragement along the way. Let them know that you believe in their abilities and are there to help them succeed.

4....**Celebrate Progress**..: Acknowledge and celebrate their progress, no matter how small. Positive reinforcement can go a long way in boosting motivation.

5....**Offer Training and Development**..: Sometimes demotivation can stem from feeling stagnant or unchallenged. Offer opportunities for training and development to help them learn new skills and grow professionally.

6...**Encourage Self-Care**..: Remind them of the importance of self-care and taking breaks when needed. Encourage activities that promote relaxation and well-being, such as exercise, meditation, or spending time with loved ones.

7....**Provide Feedback**..: Offer constructive feedback to help them improve and grow. Be specific about what they are doing well and where they can make improvements.

**8...Create a Positive Environment..:** Foster a positive work or social environment where individuals feel valued and supported. Encourage teamwork and collaboration, and recognize the contributions of each team member.

**9...Lead by Example..:** Be a positive role model by demonstrating motivation and enthusiasm in your own work. Your attitude and actions can inspire others to do the same.

**10...Seek Professional Help if needed..:** If demotivation persists and starts to affect their well-being or performance, encourage them to seek professional help from a counselor or therapist who specializes in motivational issues.

Remember, each person is unique, so it may take some trial and error to find the strategies that work best for them. Patience, empathy, and ongoing support are key in helping demotivated individuals regain their motivation and confidence.

# Chapter 5:

## Learning

## Infinite Advantages of Learning: A Comprehensive Exploration

## Introduction:

In a world defined by constant change and evolution, learning stands as the bedrock of progress and development. From the earliest stages of human civilization to the digital age of today, the pursuit of knowledge has been central to our advancement as a species. Learning is not merely a means to an end but a lifelong journey, offering numerous advantages that extend far beyond the acquisition of skills or information. In this comprehensive exploration, we delve into the multifaceted benefits of learning, ranging from personal growth and professional success to societal progress and cultural enrichment.

## Part 1: The Personal Advantages of Learning

### 1.1 Cognitive Development:

- Learning stimulates cognitive functions, enhancing memory, problem-solving abilities, and critical thinking skills.

- Continuous learning fosters neuroplasticity, promoting brain health and reducing the risk of cognitive decline with age.

- Through challenging our minds with new information and experiences, we expand our intellectual capacities and adaptability.

### 1.2 Personal Growth:

- Learning fuels personal growth by encouraging self-reflection, introspection, and the exploration of one's interests and passions.

- It fosters a sense of curiosity and wonder, leading to greater fulfillment and satisfaction in life

.

- The process of learning often involves overcoming obstacles and setbacks, fostering resilience and perseverance.

## 1.3 Emotional Well-being:

- Engaging in learning activities can boost self-esteem and confidence as individuals develop new skills and knowledge.

- Learning provides an outlet for self-expression and creativity, contributing to a sense of purpose and fulfillment.

- It offers opportunities for social interaction and connection, reducing feelings of isolation and loneliness.

## Part 2: The Professional Advantages of Learning

## 2.1 Career Advancement:

- Continuous learning is essential for staying competitive in today's rapidly evolving job market.

- Acquiring new skills and knowledge opens doors to career advancement opportunities and increased earning potential.

- Employers value employees who demonstrate a commitment to learning and professional development, leading to greater job security and satisfaction.

## 2.2 Adaptability:

- Learning equips individuals with the flexibility and adaptability needed to thrive in dynamic work environments.

- It enables workers to stay abreast of industry trends, technological advancements, and changing market demands.

- Lifelong learners are better equipped to pivot and transition between different roles or industries as needed.

## 2.3 Innovation and Problem-solving:

- Learning fosters innovation by encouraging individuals to think creatively, challenge conventional wisdom, and explore new ideas.

- It cultivates problem-solving skills, enabling individuals to identify and address complex challenges in the workplace.

- Organizations that prioritize a culture of learning are more likely to innovate and adapt to changing circumstances, gaining a competitive edge in the marketplace.

## Part 3: The Societal Advantages of Learning

## 3.1 Economic Growth:

- A well-educated workforce drives economic growth and prosperity by fueling innovation, productivity, and entrepreneurship.

- Investment in education and lifelong learning initiatives leads to higher employment rates, increased earning potential, and reduced income inequality.

- Learning contributes to the development of human capital, which is essential for sustainable economic development in the long run.

## 3.2 Social Cohesion:

- Learning fosters social cohesion by promoting empathy, understanding, and cooperation among individuals from diverse backgrounds.

- Education plays a crucial role in promoting tolerance, diversity, and inclusivity, thereby reducing social tensions and conflicts.

- Lifelong learning initiatives that cater to marginalized or underserved communities help bridge socioeconomic divides and promote social equity.

## 3.3 Civic Engagement:

- Educated individuals are more likely to participate in civic and political activities, such as voting, volunteering, and community organizing.

- Learning empowers citizens to make informed decisions and advocate for positive social change within their communities.

- A well-educated populace is essential for the functioning of democratic societies, ensuring active participation in governance and policymaking processes.

## Part 4: The Cultural Advantages of Learning

## 4.1 Preservation and Appreciation:

- Learning allows individuals to explore and appreciate diverse cultures, languages, and traditions from around the world.

- It fosters a sense of cultural awareness and respect, leading to greater tolerance and acceptance of cultural differences.

- Education plays a vital role in preserving cultural heritage and traditions for future generations, preventing their loss or erosion over time.

## 4.2 Creative Expression:

- Through the arts, literature, and humanities, learning provides opportunities for creative expression and cultural enrichment.

- It encourages individuals to explore their creativity, imagination, and unique perspectives, contributing to the richness of cultural expression.

- Cultural learning fosters cross-cultural dialogue and collaboration, bridging divides and fostering mutual understanding among diverse communities.

Learning is not merely a means to an end but a transformative journey that enriches our lives on multiple levels. From personal growth and professional success to societal progress and cultural enrichment, the advantages of learning are infinite and far-reaching. By embracing a lifelong commitment to learning, we not only empower ourselves but also contribute to a brighter and more prosperous future for all. As the poet William Butler Yeats once said, "Education is not the filling of a pail, but the lighting of a fire." Let us ignite the flames of curiosity, discovery, and lifelong learning, illuminating the path to a better world for generations to come.

## Theories of Learning

Exploring theories of learning involves delving into diverse perspectives, from cognitive to Behavior al, constructivist to sociocultural. Each theory offers unique insights into how individuals acquire knowledge, skills, and Behavior s. Here's an overview of some prominent theories of learning:

## 1...Behaviorism..:

- ..Key Figures..: Ivan Pavlov, John B. Watson, B.F. Skinner

- ..Core Tenets..: Behaviorism posits that learning is a result of stimulus-response associations. Individuals learn through conditioning, either classical (Pavlovian) or operant (Skinnerian).

- ..Implications..: Behavior ist approaches emphasize observable Behavior s and often employ reinforcement and punishment to shape Behavior.

- ..Critiques..: Critics argue that Behaviorism oversimplifies complex human learning processes, neglecting cognitive aspects and internal mental processes.

## 2...Cognitive Theory..:

- ..Key Figures..: Jean Piaget, Lev Vygotsky

- ..Core Tenets..: Cognitive theories focus on internal mental processes, such as memory, problem-solving, and information processing. Piaget's theory emphasizes stages of cognitive development, while Vygotsky's socio-cultural theory highlights the role of social interaction and cultural context in learning.

- ..Implications..: Cognitive approaches advocate for active engagement, scaffolding, and promoting higher-order thinking skills.

- ..Critiques..: Critics argue that cognitive theories may overlook the influence of emotions, motivation, and individual differences in learning.

### 3...Constructivism..:

- ..Key Figures..: Jerome Bruner, Lev Vygotsky

- ..Core Tenets..: Constructivism posits that learners actively construct their own understanding of the world by integrating new knowledge with existing knowledge and experiences. Learning is viewed as a meaning-making process.

- ..Implications..: Constructivist approaches emphasize hands-on, experiential learning, collaborative activities, and the use of authentic tasks.

- ..Critiques..: Critics raise concerns about the potential lack of structure and guidance in purely constructivist approaches and the difficulty of objectively assessing learning outcomes.

### 4. ..Social Learning Theory..:

- ..Key Figures..: Albert Bandura

- ..Core Tenets..: Social learning theory suggests that learning occurs through observation, imitation, and modeling of others. Individuals learn not only through direct experiences but also by observing the Behavior  of others and the consequences of those Behavior s.

- ..Implications..: Social learning theory highlights the importance of role models, peer influence, and media in shaping Behavior .

- ..Critiques..: Critics argue that social learning theory may oversimplify the complexities of human Behavior and underestimate the role of internal factors.

### 5...Connectivism..:

- ..Key Figures..: George Siemens, Stephen Downes

- ..Core Tenets..: Connectivism is a learning theory for

the digital age, proposing that learning is distributed across networks of people and technology. It emphasizes the importance of building and navigating networks, accessing and evaluating information, and adapting to rapid changes in knowledge landscapes.

- ..Implications..: Connectivist approaches focus on digital literacies, networked learning environments, and the cultivation of critical thinking and sense-making skills.

- ..Critiques..: Critics question the applicability of connectivism to all learning contexts, particularly those that are not heavily reliant on digital technologies.

## 6...Humanistic Theory..:

- ..Key Figures..: Abraham Maslow, Carl Rogers

- ..Core Tenets..: Humanistic theories of learning emphasize the holistic development of individuals, focusing on self-actualization, personal growth, and fulfillment of one's potential. Learning is viewed as a self-directed and inherently meaningful process.

- ..Implications..: Humanistic approaches prioritize learner autonomy, authenticity, and the creation of supportive learning environments that foster creativity and emotional well-being.

- ..Critiques..: Critics argue that humanistic theories may lack practical strategies for instructional design and assessment and may not adequately address the role of social and cultural factors in learning.

## 7...Experiential Learning..:

- ..Key Figures..: David Kolb

- ..Core Tenets..: Experiential learning theory proposes that learning is a continuous cycle involving concrete experiences, reflective observation, abstract conceptualization, and active experimentation. Learning is enhanced when individuals actively engage in experiences and reflect on the outcomes.

- ..Implications..: Experiential learning approaches emphasize hands-on activities, real-world applications, and reflective practices.

- ..Critiques..: Critics raise concerns about the transferability of learning from specific experiences to broader contexts and the potential for bias in reflective processes.


**8...Information Processing Theory..:**

- ..Key Figures..: George A. Miller, Richard Atkinson, Alan Baddeley

- ..Core Tenets..: Information processing theory draws analogies between the human mind and computer systems, viewing learning as the processing and storage of information. It focuses on how individuals perceive, encode, store, and retrieve information.


- ..Implications..: Information processing approaches emphasize strategies for improving memory, attention, and problem-solving skills through techniques such as chunking, rehearsal, and elaboration.

- ..Critiques..: Critics argue that information processing theory may oversimplify the complexities of human cognition and neglect the influence of emotions, motivations, and sociocultural factors on learning.

## 9...Multiple Intelligences Theory..:

- ..Key Figures..: Howard Gardner

- ..Core Tenets..: Multiple intelligences theory proposes that intelligence is not a unitary trait but rather a collection of distinct abilities or intelligences, including linguistic, logical-mathematical, spatial, musical, bodily-kinesthetic, interpersonal, intrapersonal, and naturalistic intelligences.

- ..Implications..: Multiple intelligences theory advocates for personalized and diverse instructional strategies that cater to the varied strengths and interests of learners.

- ..Critiques..: Critics question the empirical evidence supporting the existence of discrete intelligences and the practicality of implementing individualized instruction in educational settings.


## 10...Motivation Theories..:

- ..Key Figures..: Abraham Maslow, B.F. Skinner, Edward Deci, Richard Ryan

- ..Core Tenets..: Motivation theories seek to understand the factors that drive and sustain Behavior including intrinsic (internal) and extrinsic (external) motivators. These theories explore concepts such as needs, rewards, goals, self-efficacy, and autonomy.

- ..Implications..: Motivation theories inform instructional practices by highlighting the importance of creating engaging learning experiences, providing meaningful feedback, and fostering a supportive learning environment.

- ..Critiques..: Critics argue that motivation theories may oversimplify the complexities of human motivation and overlook the dynamic interplay between individual, social, and contextual factors.

In conclusion, theories of learning offer valuable frameworks for understanding how learning occurs and guiding educational practices. While each theory has its strengths and limitations, a holistic approach that integrates insights from multiple perspectives can provide a more comprehensive understanding of learning processes and inform effective teaching and learning strategies.

Remedies to enhance Learning skills

Title: Enhancing Learning Skills: Strategies and Techniques for Academic Success

Introduction:

Learning is a dynamic process that involves acquiring knowledge, skills, and attitudes through various experiences. Enhancing learning skills is essential for academic success and personal development. In today's fast-paced world, where information is readily available and constantly evolving, individuals need effective strategies and techniques to optimize their learning potential. This essay explores the importance of enhancing learning skills, examines key strategies and techniques for improving learning outcomes, and discusses the role of motivation and mindset in the learning process.

### Importance of Enhancing Learning Skills:

**Enhancing learning skills is crucial for several reasons:**

**1. Academic Success**: Improved learning skills lead to better academic performance. Students who develop effective study habits, critical thinking abilities, and problem-solving skills are more likely to excel in their studies.

**2. Lifelong Learning**: Learning is not confined to the classroom; it is a lifelong journey. Individuals who continually enhance their learning skills are better equipped to adapt to new challenges, acquire new knowledge, and pursue personal and professional growth throughout their lives.

**3. Career Advancement**: In today's competitive job market, employers value individuals who possess strong learning skills. Continuous learning and skill development are essential for career advancement and staying relevant in rapidly changing industries.

**4. Personal Development**: Enhancing learning skills fosters personal development by encouraging self-reflection, curiosity, and intellectual growth. It enhances one's ability to understand oneself and the world, leading to greater self-awareness and fulfillment.

## Strategies for Enhancing Learning Skills:

**1. Active Learning**: Active learning engages students in the learning process through activities such as discussions, problem-solving, and hands-on experiences. This approach promotes deeper understanding, retention, and application of knowledge compared to passive learning methods like listening to lectures.

**2. Effective Time Management**: Time management is crucial for effective learning. Students should prioritize tasks, set realistic goals, and allocate time efficiently for studying, assignments, and other responsibilities. Techniques such as the Pomodoro Technique, which involves working in short bursts with breaks in between, can improve focus and productivity.

**3. Note-Taking Strategies**: Effective note-taking enhances comprehension and retention of information. Students should develop strategies such as summarizing key points, organizing information using outlines or mind maps, and actively engaging with the material by asking questions and making connections.

**4. Critical Thinking Skills**: Critical thinking involves analyzing information, evaluating arguments, and forming reasoned judgments. Students can enhance their critical thinking skills by practicing techniques such as questioning assumptions, considering alternative perspectives, and applying logical reasoning to solve problems.

**5. Memory Techniques**: Memory plays a crucial role in learning. Students can improve their memory through techniques such as spaced repetition, mnemonics, and visualization. These techniques help encode information more effectively and retrieve it when needed.

**6. Collaborative Learning**: Collaborative learning involves working with peers to achieve common learning goals. It promotes teamwork, communication skills, and peer support, leading to deeper understanding and shared knowledge.

**7. Utilizing Resources**: Students should make use of various resources to enhance their learning experience, including textbooks, online courses, academic journals, and educational websites. Libraries, study groups, and tutoring services are also valuable resources for academic support.

**8. Reflection and Feedback**: Reflection allows students to evaluate their learning progress, identify areas for improvement, and set goals for future learning. Seeking feedback from peers, instructors, or mentors provides valuable insights and helps students gain perspective on their strengths and weaknesses.

## Motivation and Mindset in Learning:

Motivation and mindset play critical roles in the learning process:

**1. Intrinsic Motivation**: Intrinsic motivation, driven by internal factors such as curiosity, interest, and passion, is associated with higher levels of engagement and persistence in learning. Students who are intrinsically motivated are more likely to set challenging goals, take initiative, and enjoy the learning process.

**2. Extrinsic Motivation**: Extrinsic motivation, stemming from external rewards or consequences, can also influence learning Behavior . While rewards such as grades or praise can provide temporary incentives, intrinsic motivation is considered more sustainable for long-term learning success.

**3. Growth Mindset**: A growth mindset is the belief that abilities and intelligence can be developed through effort, perseverance, and learning from failure. Students with a growth mindset embrace challenges, view setbacks as opportunities for growth, and are more resilient in the face of obstacles.

**4. Fixed Mindset**: In contrast, a fixed mindset is the belief that abilities are innate and cannot be changed. Students with a fixed mindset may avoid challenges, give up easily when faced with difficulties, and perceive failure as evidence of their lack of ability.

**5. Cultivating a Growth Mindset**: Educators and parents play a crucial role in fostering a growth mindset in students. Encouraging a learning-oriented environment, providing constructive feedback and emphasizing the importance of effort and persistence can help cultivate a growth mindset and enhance learning outcomes.

## Conclusion:

Enhancing learning skills is essential for academic success, personal development, and lifelong learning. By adopting effective strategies and techniques such as active learning, time management, critical thinking, and memory techniques, individuals can optimize their learning potential and achieve their goals. Moreover, motivation and mindset play significant roles in shaping learning Behavior and attitudes. Cultivating intrinsic motivation and a growth mindset can empower individuals to overcome challenges, persist in their learning journey, and realize their full potential. Ultimately, by investing in the enhancement of learning skills, individuals can unlock new opportunities, broaden their horizons, and thrive in an ever-changing world.

# Chapter 6:

## Behavior

## Understanding Human Behavior

# Introduction

Human Behavior is a complex interplay of various factors, encompassing genetics, environment, culture, and personal experiences. It is a dynamic field of study that has intrigued scientists, psychologists, sociologists, and philosophers for centuries. From ancient times to modern research, humans have sought to comprehend the intricacies of why we act the way we do, how we interact with others, and what influences our decisions.

This introduction serves as a gateway into the vast realm of human Behavior providing an overview of its significance, the disciplines that study it, key theories, and the methodologies employed in its exploration.

## 1. Significance of Studying Human Behavior:

Understanding human Behavior  is crucial for several reasons. Firstly, it aids in improving interpersonal relationships, whether in personal, professional, or social settings. By comprehending the motivations and actions of oneself and others, individuals can navigate social interactions more effectively, leading to enhanced communication and collaboration.

Secondly, studying human Behavior is essential for addressing societal challenges. Issues such as crime, poverty, addiction, and mental health disorders are deeply rooted in human Behavior. By delving into the underlying causes and mechanisms, researchers can develop interventions and policies aimed at promoting positive change and improving well-being on both individual and societal levels.

Furthermore, insights into human Behavior are invaluable in fields such as marketing, economics, politics, and education. Businesses use consumer Behavior analysis to tailor their products and services, while policymakers rely on Behavior al economics to design more effective public policies. Educators incorporate principles of learning and motivation to optimize teaching strategies and enhance student engagement.

## 2. Disciplines Studying Human Behavior:

Human Behavior is a multidimensional phenomenon studied from various perspectives. Major disciplines include:

- **Psychology**: Psychology is the scientific study of the mind and Behavior. It encompasses a broad range of subfields, including clinical psychology, cognitive psychology, developmental psychology, social psychology, and neuroscience. Psychologists employ diverse methodologies, such as experiments, surveys, and observational studies, to explore different aspects of human Behavior.

- **Sociology**: Sociology focuses on the study of society, including social institutions, relationships, and structures. Sociologists examine how social factors influence human Behavior including culture, social norms, inequality, and social change. Research methods in sociology include surveys, interviews, ethnography, and statistical analysis.

- **Anthropology**: Anthropology investigates human Behavior within the context of culture and evolution. It encompasses cultural anthropology, which examines the beliefs, practices, and customs of different societies, as well as biological anthropology, archaeology, and linguistic anthropology. Anthropologists use a combination of fieldwork, archival research, and laboratory analysis to understand human Behavior across time and space.

- **Economics**: Economics explores human Behavior through the lens of decision-making and resource allocation. Behavior al economics, a subfield of economics, integrates insights from psychology to examine how cognitive biases and heuristics influence economic choices. Economists use mathematical models, experiments, and data analysis to study individual and collective Behavior in markets and other economic systems.

- **Neuroscience**: Neuroscience investigates the biological basis of Behavior focusing on the structure and function of the nervous system. By studying the brain and its neural circuits, neuroscientists seek to unravel the mechanisms underlying perception, cognition, emotion, and Behavior. Techniques such as brain imaging, electrophysiology, and genetic manipulation enable researchers to explore the neural correlates of human Behavior.

## 3. Key Theories of Human Behavior:

Numerous theories have been proposed to explain and predict human Behavior across different contexts. Some of the most influential theories include:

- **Freud's Psychodynamic Theory**: Sigmund Freud proposed that human Behavior is influenced by unconscious drives and conflicts, stemming from early childhood experiences. According to Freud, personality consists of three components: the id, ego, and superego, which interact to shape Behavior.

- **Skinner's Behaviorism**: B.F. Skinner's Behavior ist theory emphasizes the role of environmental stimuli and reinforcement in shaping Behavior. According to Behaviorism, individuals learn through operant conditioning, wherein Behavior s are strengthened or weakened by their consequences.

- **Piaget's Theory of Cognitive Development**: Jean Piaget's theory posits that human Behavior  develops through stages of cognitive development, characterized by distinct ways of understanding the world. Piaget identified four stages: sensorimotor, preoperational, concrete operational and formal operational, each marked by specific cognitive abilities and limitations.

- **Bandura's Social Learning Theory**: Albert Bandura's theory highlights the role of observation and imitation in learning and Behavior. According to social learning theory, individuals acquire new Behavior s by observing others, modeling their actions, and experiencing reinforcement or punishment.

 **Maslow's Hierarchy of Needs**: Abraham Maslow proposed a hierarchical model of human needs, ranging from basic physiological needs to higher-level needs for self-actualization and transcendence. According to Maslow, individuals strive to satisfy these needs in a sequential manner, with higher-order needs becoming salient once lower-order needs are met.

## 4. Methodologies in Studying Human Behavior :

Research on human Behavior employs a variety of methodologies to collect, analyze, and interpret data. Common methodologies include:

- **Experimental Research**: Experimental studies manipulate variables to examine cause-and-effect relationships between them. Researchers control conditions to isolate the effects of specific factors on Behavior often using random assignment to ensure the validity of findings.

- **Survey Research**: Surveys collect data from a sample of individuals through self-report measures, such as questionnaires or interviews. Surveys are used to gather information about attitudes, beliefs, Behavior s, and demographics across diverse populations.

- **Observational Research**: Observational studies involve systematically observing and recording Behavior in naturalistic settings. Researchers may use structured observation protocols or unobtrusive observation methods to study Behavior without interfering with it.

- **Case Study Research**: Case studies examine specific individuals, groups, or phenomena in-depth, often using multiple sources of data, such as interviews, observations, and archival records. Case studies provide detailed insights into complex Behavior s and unique circumstances.

- **Neuroimaging Techniques**: Neuroscience research utilizes various neuroimaging techniques, such as functional magnetic resonance imaging (FMRI), electroencephalography (EEG), and positron emission tomography (PET), to visualize and measure brain activity associated with specific Behavior s or cognitive processes.

Human Behavior is a multifaceted domain of inquiry that transcends disciplinary boundaries, drawing upon insights from psychology, sociology, anthropology, economics, neuroscience, and other fields. By understanding the complexities of human Behavior researchers can address pressing societal challenges, enhance interpersonal relationships, and improve individual well-being. This introduction provides a glimpse into the vast landscape of human Behavior laying the groundwork for further exploration and inquiry into this fascinating subject.

## Theories of Human behaviour

Exploring theories of human Behavior is a vast endeavor encompassing disciplines such as psychology, sociology, anthropology, neuroscience, and economics, among others. In 3000 words, we'll delve into some key theories that attempt to explain the complexities of human Behavior.

### ... 1. Evolutionary Theory of Behavior

Central to evolutionary theory is the idea that human Behavior like all biological traits, has evolved through natural selection. This theory posits that Behavior s which conferred survival and reproductive advantages to our ancestors were more likely to be passed on to subsequent generations.

One prominent concept within evolutionary psychology is kin selection, which suggests that Behavior s that benefit relatives who share genetic material are favored by natural selection. This can explain phenomena such as altruism towards close relatives.

Moreover, evolutionary psychology offers insights into mating Behavior s, suggesting that men and women have evolved different strategies due to differences in reproductive investment. Men, with a lower investment in reproduction, are theorized to seek multiple partners to maximize their reproductive success, while women, who invest more heavily in each offspring, are more selective in their choice of mates.

## ... 2. Behaviorism

Behaviorism, popularized by psychologists like B.F. Skinner, focuses on observable Behavior s rather than internal mental processes. It suggests that Behavior  is learned through conditioning, where stimuli in the environment trigger responses.

Classical conditioning, pioneered by Ivan Pavlov, involves associating an involuntary response with a stimulus. For instance, Pavlov's dogs learned to salivate at the sound of a bell after it was repeatedly paired with food.

Operant conditioning, introduced by Skinner, involves learning through consequences. Behavior s that are reinforced (rewarded) are more likely to be repeated, while those that are punished are less likely to occur again. This theory has practical applications in various fields, from education to parenting to animal training.

## ... 3. Social Learning Theory

Social learning theory, proposed by Albert Bandura, expands upon Behaviorism by incorporating the role of cognitive processes in learning. It emphasizes the importance of observation and modeling in the acquisition of Behavior.

According to this theory, individuals learn by observing others and imitating their Behavior s. Moreover, they also learn from the consequences experienced by others, known as vicarious reinforcement or punishment. Bandura's famous Bobo doll experiment demonstrated how children imitated aggressive Behavior s they observed in adults.

## ... 4. Cognitive Theory

Cognitive theories of Behavior focus on how internal mental processes such as perception, memory, and problem-solving influence Behavior. These theories posit that individuals actively process information from their environment and use it to guide their actions.

Cognitive-Behavior al therapy (CBT), based on the work of Aaron Beck and Albert Ellis, is a widely used therapeutic approach that addresses dysfunctional thoughts and Behavior s. It suggests that maladaptive Behavior s are often the result of distorted thinking patterns and by changing these cognitions, individuals can change their Behavior s and emotions.

## ... 5. Psychoanalytic Theory

Developed by Sigmund Freud, psychoanalytic theory emphasizes the role of unconscious processes in shaping Behavior. Freud proposed that human Behavior is driven by unconscious desires and conflicts, particularly those related to sexuality and aggression.

Freud's structural model of personality includes the id, ego, and superego. The id operates on the pleasure principle, seeking immediate gratification of primal urges. The ego, guided by the reality principle, mediates between the id's demands and the constraints of reality. The superego represents internalized societal and parental standards, acting as a moral conscience.

## ... 6. Humanistic Theory

Humanistic psychology, spearheaded by Carl Rogers and Abraham Maslow, emphasizes personal growth, self-actualization, and the inherent goodness of individuals. It contrasts with earlier psychodynamic and Behavior ist approaches by focusing on subjective experiences and the importance of free will.

According to humanistic theory, individuals have an innate drive towards self-actualization, the realization of one's full potential. However, this process can be inhibited by environmental factors or negative self-concepts. Humanistic therapy aims to facilitate self-exploration and personal growth by providing a supportive and empathetic therapeutic environment.

## ... 7. Socio-Cultural Theory

Socio-cultural theory, influenced by Lev Vygotsky, emphasizes the role of social interactions and cultural context in shaping Behavior  and cognitive development. Vygotsky proposed the concept of the zone of proximal development (ZPD), which refers to the gap between what a learner can accomplish independently and what they can achieve with the guidance of a more knowledgeable other.

This theory highlights the importance of cultural tools, such as language, symbols, and artifacts, in mediating cognitive processes and shaping Behavior . It suggests that individuals learn and develop within the socio-cultural contexts in which they are embedded and that cultural value and norms influence Behavior  and cognition.

## ... 8. Biological Theory

Biological theories of Behavior  focus on the biological substrates underlying human Behavior  including genetics, neurochemistry, and neuroanatomy. These theories posit that Behavior  is influenced by biological factors such as genes, hormones, and brain structure and function.

For example, Behavior al genetics explores the role of genetic variation in individual differences in Behavior . Twin and adoption studies have been used to estimate the heritability of traits and disorders, revealing the complex interplay between genes and environment.

Neuroscience has also contributed to our understanding of Behavior  by elucidating the neural mechanisms underlying various psychological processes. Techniques such as functional magnetic resonance imaging (FMRI) and electroencephalography (EEG) allow researchers to investigate how different brain regions are involved in perception, emotion, decision-making, and other aspects of Behavior.

Theories of human Behavior offer diverse perspectives on the complex interplay of biological, cognitive, social, and cultural factors that shape who we are and how we behave. While each theory has its strengths and limitations, together they contribute to a richer understanding of human nature and Behavior . By integrating insights from multiple theoretical frameworks, researchers and practitioners can develop more comprehensive models of Behavior  and more effective interventions to promote well-being and positive social change.

# Chapter 7:

## Conflict

..Exploring Conflict: Understanding its Nature, Causes, and Resolutions..

## ..Introduction...

Conflict is an inherent aspect of human interaction and societal dynamics. From interpersonal disagreements to international disputes, conflict permeates various facets of human existence. Its multifaceted nature makes it a rich subject of study across disciplines such as psychology, sociology, political science, and anthropology. This essay aims to delve into the complex phenomenon of conflict, examining its nature, causes, manifestations, and potential resolutions.

## ..Understanding Conflict..

At its core, conflict can be defined as a clash of interests, values, or perspectives between two or more parties. This clash may arise from competing goals, scarce resources, differences in beliefs or ideologies, or simply misunderstandings. Conflict is not inherently negative; it can serve as a catalyst for growth, change, and innovation. However, unresolved or mismanaged conflict can lead to tension, hostility, and even violence.

## ..Types of Conflict...

Conflict can manifest in various forms, ranging from interpersonal conflicts between individuals to large-scale conflicts between nations. Some common types of conflict include:

1. **..Interpersonal Conflict..**: Arising between individuals due to differences in personalities, goals, or communication styles. Examples include conflicts between family members, colleagues, or friends.

2. **..Intergroup Conflict..**: Occurring within a group or organization, often stemming from disagreements over roles, responsibilities, or decision-making processes.

3. **..Intergroup Conflict..**: Emerging between different groups or communities, often fueled by competition for resources, territory, or power. Examples include ethnic conflicts, religious conflicts, or conflicts between rival factions.

4. **..Organizational Conflict..**: Arising within an organization due to disputes over policies, procedures, leadership, or resources. This type of conflict can hinder productivity and morale if not addressed effectively.

5. **..Interstate Conflict..**: Referring to conflicts between sovereign states, which can range from diplomatic tensions to full-scale warfare. Historical examples include the World Wars and the Cold War.

## ..Causes of Conflict...

The causes of conflict are diverse and multifaceted, often stemming from a combination of individual, interpersonal, societal, and structural factors. Some common causes of conflict include:

1...**Miscommunication**..: Poor communication or misunderstandings can lead to conflict by exacerbating differences and creating confusion.

2...**Competition**..: Competition for resources, status, or power can fuel conflict, especially when resources are scarce or unequally distributed.

**3...Inequality..**: Social, economic, or political inequality can breed resentment and tension, leading to conflicts between privileged and marginalized groups.

**4...Divergent Interests..**: Conflicting goals, values, or interests between parties can result in conflict as each seeks to advance their own agenda.

**5...Historical Grievances..**: Past injustices, traumas, or conflicts can create long-lasting resentments and animosities that fuel present-day conflicts.

**6...Lack of Trust..**: A lack of trust between parties can undermine cooperation and escalate conflicts, as each side perceives the other as untrustworthy or hostile.


**..Manifestations of Conflict..**


Conflict can manifest in various ways, ranging from verbal arguments and passive-aggressive Behavior  to physical violence and warfare. The intensity and severity of conflict depend on factors such as the parties involved, the issues at stake, and the context in which the conflict occurs. Some common manifestations of conflict include:


**1...Verbal Conflict..**: Arguments, debates, or verbal exchanges characterized by disagreement, criticism, or hostility.

**2...Nonverbal Conflict..**: Body language, facial expressions, or gestures that convey hostility, contempt, or defiance.

**3. ..Emotional Conflict..**: Conflicts that evoke strong emotions such as anger, fear, or resentment, making resolution challenging.

**4. ..Structural Conflict..**: Systemic or institutionalized inequalities, injustices, or power imbalances that perpetuate conflict over time.

5. ..**Physical Conflict**..: Violence, aggression, or physical confrontations resulting in harm or injury to individuals or groups.

6. ..**Psychological Conflict**..: Inner turmoil, cognitive dissonance, or psychological distress resulting from unresolved conflicts or cognitive biases.


..**Resolution of Conflict**...


While conflict is inevitable, effective conflict resolution strategies can help manage, mitigate, or resolve conflicts in constructive ways. Some common approaches to conflict resolution include:


1...**Communication**..: Open, honest, and respectful communication can help parties understand each other's perspectives, clarify misunderstandings, and find common ground.

2...**Negotiation**..: Diplomatic negotiation involves bargaining, compromise, and problem-solving to reach mutually acceptable agreements.

3...**Mediation**..: A neutral third party facilitates communication and negotiation between conflicting parties, helping them finds mutually beneficial solutions.

4...**Conflict Transformation**..: Transformative approaches focus on addressing underlying causes of conflict, promoting reconciliation, and fostering positive social change.

5...**Conflict Management**..: Proactive management strategies aim to prevent conflicts from escalating, such as implementing clear policies, fostering a culture of respect, and promoting conflict resolution skills.

**6...Restorative Justice**..: Restorative approaches focus on repairing harm, promoting healing, and restoring relationships between parties affected by conflict.

Conflict is a pervasive and complex phenomenon that shapes human interactions, relationships, and societies. While conflict is inevitable, it is not inherently destructive; when managed effectively, conflict can lead to growth, understanding, and positive change. By understanding the nature, causes, and manifestations of conflict, and by employing appropriate conflict resolution strategies, individuals, communities, and nations can navigate conflicts in ways that promote peace, justice, and reconciliation.

The impact of conflict on society is profound and multifaceted, shaping the course of history, altering socio -political structures, and influencing the lives of individuals in myriad ways. Conflict, whether internal or external, armed or ideological, has been a persistent feature of human civilization since time immemorial. From ancient tribal conflicts to modern-day wars, the effects of conflict reverberate through generations, leaving indelible marks on societies worldwide.

To comprehensively understand the effects of conflict on society, it's essential to examine its various dimensions, including social, economic, political, and psychological aspects. In this exploration, we'll delve into these dimensions to illuminate the intricate ways in which conflict shapes societies.

**..1. Social Effects of Conflict:**

At the social level, conflict can lead to profound disruptions in communities, tearing apart the fabric of society and exacerbating divisions among people. One of the most immediate consequences of conflict is displacement, as people flee violence and seek refuge elsewhere. This displacement can result in the breakdown of social networks and the loss of cultural identity as communities are uprooted from their ancestral lands.

Moreover, conflict often breeds distrust and hostility among different ethnic, religious, or ideological groups, fueling sectarian violence and deepening societal rifts. Prejudice, discrimination, and intolerance may become rampant as people seek scapegoats for the hardships wrought by conflict. In extreme cases, conflicts can escalate into genocide or ethnic cleansing, leading to mass atrocities and irrevocable trauma for affected populations.

On the other hand, conflict can also galvanize solidarity and foster resilience within communities. In the face of adversity, people may come together to support one another, forging bonds that transcend traditional divisions. Grassroots movements for peace and reconciliation often emerge from the crucible of conflict, advocating for dialogue and understanding as pathways to healing societal wounds.

## ..2. Economic Effects of Conflict:

The economic consequences of conflict are profound and far-reaching, affecting not only the warring parties but also neighboring states and the global economy. Warfare destroys infrastructure, disrupts trade routes, and undermines productivity, leading to widespread poverty and economic stagnation. The diversion of resources towards military expenditure drains public coffers, diverting funds away from essential services such as healthcare, education, and social welfare.

Furthermore, conflict creates a climate of uncertainty and instability that deters foreign investment and hinders economic development. In war-torn regions, businesses may shutter their doors, and entrepreneurs flee for safer havens, exacerbating unemployment and exacerbating poverty. The informal economy often thrives amidst conflict, as people resort to illicit activities such as smuggling and black-market trade to survive.

Rebuilding economies shattered by conflict is a Herculean task that requires substantial investment, political stability, and long-term planning. International aid and development assistance play a crucial role in post-conflict reconstruction efforts, providing humanitarian relief, infrastructure development, and support for livelihoods. However, the road to economic recovery is fraught with challenges, and progress may be slow and uneven, particularly in contexts plagued by ongoing violence and political instability.

## ..3. Political Effects of Conflict:

Conflict reshapes the political landscape, altering power dynamics, and challenging existing institutions and governance structures. In some cases, conflict may lead to regime change, as popular uprisings or armed rebellions topple entrenched rulers and pave the way for new leadership. Transitional periods following conflict are often marked by political instability and uncertainty as rival factions vie for control and compete to shape the future direction of the state.

Moreover, conflict can exacerbate existing divisions within societies, polarizing political discourse and undermining democratic norms. Authoritarian regimes may exploit crises to consolidate power and suppress dissent, using state violence and repression to quell opposition. The erosion of civil liberties and the rule of law can have long-lasting consequences for the democratic fabric of society, curtailing freedoms and undermining trust in government institutions.

On the other hand, conflict can also serve as a catalyst for political change and social reform, mobilizing citizens to demand accountability and participatory governance. Grassroots movements for democracy and human rights often gain momentum during times of crisis, advocating for inclusive political processes and the protection of fundamental rights. International actors, such as the United Nations and regional organizations, may play a vital role in mediating conflicts and facilitating peace negotiations, offering diplomatic support and fostering dialogue between warring parties.

## ..4. Psychological Effects of Conflict:

The psychological toll of conflict on individuals and communities is immense, leaving scars that endure long after the guns fall silent. Exposure to violence, displacement, and loss can result in a range of mental health disorders, including post-traumatic stress disorder (PTSD), depression, and anxiety. Children are particularly vulnerable to the psychological effects of conflict, as they may experience disrupted education, family separation, and exposure to traumatic events that can have lasting repercussions on their emotional well-being.

Furthermore, conflict can perpetuate cycles of trauma and violence, as the wounds of the past continue to haunt future generations. Memories of past atrocities may fuel resentment and perpetuate intergenerational conflict, hindering efforts at reconciliation and healing. Addressing the psychological needs of survivors and providing mental health support is essential for fostering resilience and promoting long-term peace and stability.


In conclusion, the effects of conflict on society are profound and multifaceted, permeating every aspect of human life. From the social upheaval wrought by displacement and division to the economic devastation of livelihoods and infrastructure, conflict leaves a trail of destruction in its wake. Yet, amidst the chaos and despair, there are also opportunities for resilience, solidarity, and renewal. By addressing the root causes of conflict, promoting dialogue and reconciliation, and investing in peacebuilding efforts, societies can chart a path towards a more peaceful and prosperous future.

# Chapter 8:

Social Psychology and Human Being

Understanding Social Psychology: Exploring Human Behavior in Social Contexts

# Introduction

Social psychology is the scientific study of how individuals think, feel, and behave in social contexts. It examines the influence of social factors on human Behavior cognition, and emotions. This field delves into a wide array of topics, including conformity, obedience, group dynamics, prejudice, interpersonal attraction, aggression, and altruism. By understanding the mechanisms underlying social Behavior  social psychologists aim to unravel the complexities of human interactions and contribute to improving societal well-being.

# Historical Overview

The roots of social psychology can be traced back to the late 19th century when psychologists began to explore the impact of social influences on individual Behavior . Early experiments by researchers like Norman Triplett on social facilitation laid the groundwork for the field. However, it was the work of pioneers such as Kurt Lewin, Solomon Asch, and Stanley Milgram in the mid-20th century that established social psychology as a distinct discipline.

Lewin's field theory emphasized the importance of considering the individual within the context of their social environment, while Asch's studies on conformity demonstrated the power of group pressure on individual decision-making. Milgram's obedience experiments shed light on the extent to which individuals would comply with authority figures, even at the expense of harming others. These seminal studies provided valuable insights into the complexities of human Behavior  in social settings.

# Key Concepts in Social Psychology

**1...Social Influence**..: One of the central themes in social psychology, social influence refers to the ways in which the presence or actions of others can affect an individual's thoughts, feelings, or Behavior s. This includes phenomena such as conformity, compliance, and obedience.

**2...Conformity**..: Conformity involves adjusting one's Behavior or beliefs to align with those of a group. Asch's famous line judgment experiments demonstrated the powerful influence of social norms on individuals' willingness to go along with group consensus, even when it contradicted their own perceptions.

**3...Compliance**..: Compliance occurs when individuals change their Behavior in response to a direct request from another person. Techniques such as foot-in-the-door and door-in-the -face are commonly studied methods of achieving compliance.

**4...Obedience**..: Obedience refers to following the orders or commands of an authority figure. Milgram's obedience experiments revealed the disturbing extent to which individuals would obey authority, even when it conflicted with their moral beliefs.

**5...Group Dynamics**..: Group dynamics explores how individuals behave in groups, including topics such as leadership, decision-making, and group cohesion. Studies like Zimbardo's Stanford prison experiment highlighted the rapid formation of social roles and the potential for abuse of power within groups.

**6 ...Prejudice and Discrimination**..: Prejudice refers to negative attitudes or beliefs held about individuals based on their membership in a particular group, while discrimination involves Behavior s directed toward individuals based on their group membership. Understanding the roots of prejudice and discrimination is crucial for promoting tolerance and equality in society.

**7...Interpersonal Attraction..:** Interpersonal attraction examines the factors that influence liking and attraction between individuals. Research in this area explores variables such as physical attractiveness, similarity, and proximity.

**8...Aggression..:** Aggression encompasses a range of Behavior s intended to harm others. Social psychologists investigate the causes and consequences of aggression, as well as strategies for reducing its prevalence in society.

**9...Altruism..:** Altruism refers to selfless Behavior s that benefits others without expecting anything in return. Exploring the motivations behind altruistic acts sheds light on the underlying mechanisms of prosocial Behavior.

## Applications of Social Psychology

Social psychology has numerous practical applications across various domains, including health, business, education, and public policy. For example:

**1...Health Psychology..:** Social psychological principles are used to promote healthy Behavior s, such as smoking cessation, exercise adherence, and vaccination uptake. Interventions that leverage social norms and social support can be effective in promoting positive health outcomes.

**2...Consumer Behavior ..:** Understanding the psychological factors that influence consumer decision-making helps marketers develop more effective advertising strategies and product designs. Concepts such as social proof and persuasion tactics are commonly employed in marketing campaigns.

**3...Education..:** Social psychology informs teaching practices by highlighting the importance of social interactions in the learning process. Techniques such as cooperative learning and peer tutoring capitalize on social dynamics to enhance student engagement and academic achievement.

**4...Conflict Resolution..:** By understanding the psychological processes underlying intergroup conflict, social psychologists can develop strategies for promoting peace and reconciliation. Techniques such as contact theory emphasize the importance of positive interactions between conflicting groups in reducing prejudice and fostering mutual understanding.

In conclusion, social psychology offers valuable insights into the complex interplay between individuals and their social environment. By examining the mechanisms of social influence, group dynamics, prejudice, and altruism, social psychologists contribute to our understanding of human Behavior  and inform interventions aimed at improving societal well-being. As the field continues to evolve, it holds the promise of addressing pressing social issues and fostering positive social change.

Certainly! Social psychology is a fascinating field that explores how individuals' thoughts, feelings, and Behavior s are influenced by the presence of others. Within this domain, numerous tools and techniques are employed to understand and investigate various social phenomena. In this comprehensive overview, I'll delve into some of the key tools and techniques used in social psychology research, including experimental designs, survey methods, observational techniques, and more.

**..Introduction to Social Psychology Tools and Techniques..**

Social psychology is a dynamic field that employs a wide range of tools and techniques to explore human Behavior  in social contexts. From classic experiments to cutting-edge methodologies, researchers utilize various approaches to investigate the intricate workings of the human mind in social situations. In this comprehensive review, we will delve into the key tools and techniques employed in social psychology research, examining their strengths, limitations, and applications.

## ..Experimental Designs

Experimental designs are fundamental to social psychology research, allowing researchers to establish cause-and-effect relationships between variables. One of the most common experimental designs used is the randomized controlled trial (RCT)... In an RCT, participants are randomly assigned to either an experimental group, which receives a treatment or intervention, or a control group, which does not. By comparing the outcomes between the two groups, researchers can assess the effects of the treatment while controlling for potential confounding variables.

Another important experimental design is the .Quasi-experiment.., which lacks random assignment. Instead, participants are grouped based on pre-existing characteristics or conditions. While quasi-experiments are less rigorous than RCTs, they are often used in social psychology when random assignment is not feasible or ethical.

## ..Survey Methods…

Surveys are widely used in social psychology to collect data on attitudes, beliefs, and Behavior s. Surveys can be administered in various formats, including paper-and-pencil questionnaires, online surveys, and interviews. One advantage of surveys is their ability to gather large amounts of data from diverse populations quickly and efficiently.

## ..Observational Techniques…

Observational techniques involve systematically observing and recording Behavior in natural or controlled settings. One common method is ...Naturalistic observation.., where researchers observe participants in their natural environment without interference. Naturalistic observation allows researchers to study Behavior as it occurs naturally, providing valuable insights into real-world social interactions.

Another observational technique is ...Participant observation.., where researchers actively participate in the social setting they are studying. By immersing themselves in the environment, researchers can gain a deeper understanding of the social dynamics at play.

## ..Content Analysis…

Content analysis involves systematically analyzing the content of written, verbal, or visual communication. Researchers use content analysis to identify patterns, themes, and trends in media, literature, speeches, and other forms of communication. This method provides valuable insights into societal values, norms, and attitudes.

## ..Social Network Analysis…

Social network analysis (SNA) is a method for studying the structure and dynamics of social networks. Researchers use SNA to map and analyze relationships between individuals or groups, examining patterns of interaction, influence, and communication. SNA can be applied to various contexts, including organizational networks, online communities, and friendship networks.

## ..Experimental Manipulations…

Experimental manipulations involve systematically altering independent variables to observe their effects on dependent variables. Manipulations can range from subtle changes in social cues to more overt interventions. For example, researchers might manipulate the presence of bystanders to study the bystander effect or manipulate social norms to examine conformity.

## ..Psycho physiological Measures…

Psychophysiological measures assess physiological responses to social stimuli, providing insights into the underlying mechanisms of Behavior . Common psychophysiological measures include heart rate, skin conductance, and brain activity (e.g., EEG, FMRI). These measures allow researchers to study the physiological correlates of social processes such as arousal, emotion, and attention.

## ..Implicit Measures…

Implicit measures assess unconscious or automatic processes that may not be accessible to conscious awareness. One example is the ..Implicit Association Test (IAT).., which measures the strength of associations between concepts (e.g., race, gender) and evaluations (e.g., positive, negative). Implicit measures provide valuable insights into implicit biases, attitudes, and stereotypes.

## ..Computer Simulations and Modeling…

Computer simulations and modeling are increasingly used in social psychology to study complex social phenomena. These techniques involve creating computational models that simulate social interactions and dynamics. By manipulating variables and running simulations, researchers can explore how individual Behavior s give rise to emergent social patterns.

## ..Meta-Analysis…

Meta-analysis involves systematically combining and analyzing data from multiple studies to draw conclusions about a particular research question. Meta-analysis allows researchers to quantitatively synthesize findings across studies, providing more robust and reliable estimates of effect sizes. Meta-analysis is especially useful for resolving inconsistencies or discrepancies in the literature.

## ..Ethical Considerations…

Ethical considerations are paramount in social psychology research, given the potential impact on participants' well-being and rights. Researchers must obtain informed consent from participants, protect their privacy and confidentiality, and minimize any potential risks or harm. Additionally, researchers should strive to conduct research that is culturally sensitive and socially responsible.

## Conclusion…

In conclusion, social psychology employs a diverse array of tools and techniques to investigate human Behavior in social contexts. From experimental designs and survey methods to observational techniques and computer simulations, researchers utilize a range of approaches to explore the complexities of social interaction. By employing rigorous methodologies and ethical practices, social psychologists can gain valuable insights into the fundamental processes that shape our social world.

# Chapter 9:

## Role of Research in Human Psychology

Research in human psychology spans a vast array of topics, from understanding the inner workings of the mind to exploring the intricacies of social interactions. With roots in philosophy and physiology, psychology has evolved into a multifaceted discipline that employs diverse methodologies to unravel the mysteries of human Behavior and cognition. In this exploration, we will delve into some of the prominent areas of research in contemporary human psychology, ranging from cognitive psychology to social psychology, developmental psychology, clinical psychology, and beyond.


**..Cognitive Psychology: Unraveling the Mind's Mysteries..**


Cognitive psychology investigates the mental processes punderlying human Behavior  including perception, memory, attention, language, problem-solving, and decision-making. Researchers in this field employ various experimental techniques, such as Behavior al experiments, neuroimaging, and computational modeling, to uncover the mechanisms governing cognitive functions.

One significant area of research in cognitive psychology is memory. Researchers aim to understand how memories are formed, stored, and retrieved, as well as the factors that influence memory accuracy and reliability. Studies have revealed insights into the role of attention, encoding strategies, and emotional arousal in memory formation. Moreover, research in cognitive psychology has practical applications, such as improving educational practices, eyewitness testimony reliability, and developing interventions for memory disorders.

Another cornerstone of cognitive psychology is perception, which examines how individuals interpret and make sense of sensory information. Research in perception investigates topics like visual illusions, depth perception, and the perception of time. By studying perceptual processes, psychologists gain insights into how the brain constructs our subjective experience of the world around us.

## ..Social Psychology: Exploring the Dynamics of Human Interaction..

Social psychology focuses on how individuals think, feel, and behave in social contexts, exploring topics such as conformity, obedience, prejudice, aggression, altruism, and group dynamics. Researchers in this field utilize experimental methods, surveys, observations, and statistical analyses to investigate social phenomena and understand the underlying psychological mechanisms.

One area of interest in social psychology is attitudes and persuasion. Researchers examine how attitudes are formed, changed, and influenced by factors such as persuasive communication, social norms, and cognitive dissonance. Understanding these processes has implications for advertising, public health campaigns, and intergroup relations.

Another vital area of research in social psychology is interpersonal relationships. Psychologists investigate the factors that contribute to the formation, maintenance, and dissolution of relationships, as well as the dynamics of attraction, love, and intimacy. By studying relationships, researchers gain insights into human social Behavior and well-being.

## ..Developmental Psychology: Tracing the Journey from Infancy to Adulthood…

Developmental psychology explores the psychological growth and change that occurs throughout the lifespan, from infancy to old age. Researchers in this field examine cognitive, emotional, social, and physical development, aiming to understand the processes and factors that shape individuals' trajectories.

One key focus of developmental psychology is early childhood development. Researchers investigate how infants and young children acquire language, develop attachments, and form social bonds. Studying early development provides insights into the critical periods and sensitive periods that influence later psychological functioning.

Adolescence is another pivotal stage of development studied in developmental psychology. Researchers explore identity formation, peer relationships, risk-taking Behavior and the transition to adulthood. Understanding the challenges and opportunities of adolescence informs interventions aimed at promoting positive youth development.

## ..Clinical Psychology: Healing the Mind and Alleviating Psychological Distress..

Clinical psychology is concerned with the assessment, diagnosis, and treatment of mental health disorders and psychological distress. Researchers in this field investigate the causes and correlates of psychopathology, as well as the effectiveness of therapeutic interventions.

One area of research in clinical psychology is the etiology of mental disorders. Psychologists study genetic, biological, psychological, and environmental factors that contribute to the onset and maintenance of conditions such as depression, anxiety, schizophrenia, and substance use disorders. By identifying risk factors and protective factors, researchers can inform prevention and intervention efforts.

Another important focus of clinical psychology research is psychotherapy outcome and efficacy. Researchers evaluate the effectiveness of various therapeutic approaches, such as cognitive-Behavior al therapy, psychodynamic therapy, and mindfulness-based interventions. Meta-analyses and randomized controlled trials provide empirical evidence for the effectiveness of different treatment modalities.

## ..Cross-Cultural Psychology: Understanding Human Diversity and Universality..

Cross-cultural psychology examines the influence of culture on human Behavior cognition, and emotion. Researchers in this field investigate cultural differences and similarities in psychological processes, as well as the acculturation and cultural adaptation of individuals and groups.

One area of interest in cross-cultural psychology is cultural dimensions and their impact on Behavior. Psychologists like Geert Hofstede and Harry Triandis have proposed models to understand cultural variability in values, norms, and social Behavior s. Research in this area sheds light on how culture shapes individuals' attitudes, beliefs, and Behavior s.

Another important focus of cross-cultural psychology is cultural competence and diversity in mental health services. Researchers explore how cultural factors influence the expression and interpretation of psychological distress, as well as the effectiveness of therapeutic interventions across different cultural contexts. Culturally sensitive assessment and treatment approaches are essential for addressing the diverse needs of clients from various cultural backgrounds.

In conclusion, research in human psychology encompasses a broad spectrum of topics and methodologies, reflecting the complexity and diversity of human experience. From understanding the inner workings of the mind to exploring the dynamics of social interaction, developmental trajectories, mental health disorders, and cultural influences, psychologists employ a variety of approaches to advance our knowledge and improve the well-being of individuals and communities. By integrating insights from various subfields and collaborating across disciplines, researchers continue to push the boundaries of human psychology, offering new perspectives and practical solutions to the challenges we face in understanding ourselves and others.

THE DARK SKY
Dr. Hoori Nadir
THE DARK SKY
Dr. Hoori Nadir
kindle
मतदान
हमारा अधिकार
FEB 4TH 2021
WORLD
CANCER
DAY
AUTOMOTIVE
TEKNIKA
DR. RAVI MENARIA
INCIDENT OF OUR LIFE
Compiled By
Rahman Bandvi
Deepak Kumar Verma
अब नहीं तो कब ?
माँ
का प्यार
Sakshi Shukla
Introduction to
Industrial
Management
- DR. HOORI NADIR
POT
OF
INKS
COMPILED BY
JAEL KEMUMA MIGIRO
Books published from our publication .
www.bphbup.wordpress.com